TROUT

UNIVERSITY PRESS OF FLORIDA

Florida A&M University, Tallahassee
Florida Atlantic University, Boca Raton
Florida Gulf Coast University, Ft. Myers
Florida International University, Miami
Florida State University, Tallahassee
New College of Florida, Sarasota
University of Central Florida, Orlando
University of Florida, Gainesville
University of North Florida, Jacksonville
University of South Florida, Tampa
University of West Florida, Pensacola

University Press of Florida

Gainesville

Tallahassee

Tampa

Boca Raton

Pensacola

Orlando

Miami

Jacksonville

Ft. Myers

Sarasota

TROUT

A True Story of
Murder, Teens, and
the Death Penalty

JEFF KUNERTH

LIBRARY OF CONGRESS CATALOGING-IN-PUBLICATION DATA
Kunerth, Jeff.
Trout : a true story of murder, teens, and the death penalty /
Jeff Kunerth.
p. cm.
Includes bibliographical references.
ISBN 978-0-8130-3981-7 (alk. paper)
1. Juvenile delinquency—Florida. 2. Murderers—Florida—Biography.
3. Criminal investigation—Florida. 4. Capital punishment—Florida.
5. Victims of juvenile crime—Florida. I. Title.
HV9105.F7K86 2012
364.152'3092275999—dc23   2011037515

The University Press of Florida is the scholarly publishing agency for the
State University System of Florida, comprising Florida A&M University,
Florida Atlantic University, Florida Gulf Coast University, Florida
International University, Florida State University, New College of
Florida, University of Central Florida, University of Florida, University
of North Florida, University of South Florida, and University of West
Florida.

University Press of Florida
15 Northwest 15th Street
Gainesville, FL 32611-2079
http://www.upf.com

To Gretchen, for her inspiration,
encouragement, and patience

Contents

Preface

When I decided to write about a little-known murder involving three teenagers in Pensacola, Florida, in 1991, I didn't know any of the teens, their families, the victim, or his family. I had never thought much about capital punishment or juveniles in the criminal justice system. What I did know was that this would be a story about tragedy and loss: the lasting consequences of one horrible moment, one terrible mistake. It became more than that. This little-known murder, and its impact on the lives of all involved, is part of a larger debate in the United States over what should be done with juveniles who commit serious crimes. It poses the provocative question of whether juveniles engaged in crime are the same as adult criminals: if the act negates age, or if age makes a teenager less culpable for his crime.

In addressing the larger issue of juveniles and crime, this book in no way minimizes the harm inflicted on the families of Billy Wayne Coker, Stephen DuMont, Shirley Ann Cook, Gary Colley, or the other victims of violence committed by teenagers. Their pain and suffering are real and sometimes unrelenting. But in the debate over what we should do with teens who commit horrific crimes, we have to ask whether we want a criminal justice system that acts like a grieving, angry family. If we believe at all in redemption, rehabilitation, reform, and rebirth, then juveniles—the group most capable of change—should be judged and sentenced differently than adults.

TROUT

Prologue

Patrick Bonifay stepped slowly, hesitantly toward the take-out window of Trout Auto Parts. It was Friday, January 25, 1991, a few minutes before midnight. The night was cool for Pensacola, and Patrick wore a jacket and gloves. He felt the weight of a gun in the right pocket of his pants.

Daniel Wells, the man he was hired to kill, stood behind terminal seven by the window, counting the money in the cash drawer, his last task of the night. Robin Lee Archer had set it up for Patrick, explaining how he was to walk up to the window and ask Wells for a clutch part for an '85 Nissan pickup. Wells would need to go back into the warehouse to get the part, and that's when Patrick would crawl through the parts window. Shoot the man in the head, Robbie told him. Make it look like a robbery. That was the plan.

But nothing had gone according to plan Friday night. Inside the car parked outside Trout Auto on W Street were two kids Patrick had recruited to help him but whom Patrick hardly knew. Eddie Fordham was behind the wheel of the yellow Mustang he was so proud of. Patrick didn't even care much for Eddie. He knew Eddie because their girlfriends were best friends. They went to the same school, Escambia High, but Eddie was one of those rich kids who had a big house in Warrington, while Patrick grew up in a ratty trailer in rough and run-down Brownsville. Eddie was a year older, eighteen, and had his own car; Patrick didn't even have a driver's license. Patrick needed Eddie because Eddie had wheels.

In the backseat was Clifford Barth, a seventeen-year-old cousin of Patrick's best friend. Cliff was new to Pensacola. He was an Army kid whose father had recently transferred from a base in Alaska. Patrick thought Cliff was alright. Quiet. Long-haired. A pothead. Patrick doubted there was ever a time when Cliff wasn't stoned. Cliff carried a little pipe in the front pocket of his shirt. He'd whip it out throughout the day and take a couple of hits. Cliff had been along when Patrick did a couple of jobs. He was there when Patrick broke into a stereo store last December and stole audio equipment they sold for money to buy Christmas presents. When Patrick called the night before and said they could make $20,000 robbing Trout Auto Parts, Cliff said sure.

Eddie and Cliff were almost strangers. This was the first time they'd been in the same car together. Patrick had been friends with Cliff for about five months. The three boys' friendship was the quick and easy alliance that happens between teenagers who haven't yet formed attachments to a group or clique. They didn't have the mental checklist of qualities, desirable and unacceptable, that goes into adult friendships, or the parental radar that sends out warning signals when a child chooses the wrong kid to play with. It was possible at this age to be friends with a kid you didn't really like.

Eddie and Cliff waited in the car, unsure of what was going to happen, while Patrick approached the take-out window. About nine months ago, Robin Lee Archer had been fired from the store. It was a menial, low-paying job, but it provided Archer with a base from which he could sell pot and cocaine. The take-out window, which stayed open until midnight, wasn't just for selling auto parts after hours. If you came up to that window and asked for the right part, you got a baggie of weed or a packet of coke.

Since losing his job at Trout Auto, the twenty-six-year-old Archer had been sleeping on friends' couches and the front seat of his Nissan pickup. He blamed Wells for his firing. He wanted revenge, but he didn't want to exact it himself. He thought Patrick, the seventeen-year-old stepson of his cousin, might just be desperate enough, with the promise of big money, to kill a man.

Patrick *was* desperate. He hated his life. He hated his messed-up family. He hated being poor. He wanted out. He was thinking about joining the Marines with his best friend. That might be his escape. Or maybe, after tonight, he'd have enough money to marry his girlfriend and move away.

As he approached the front of Trout Auto Parts, Patrick was worried that he might not fit through the take-out window. He'd always been a little chubby. They'd made him a guard on the ninth-grade football team before he was expelled from school. He'd lost some of that weight while in a boot camp for juvenile offenders, but at five foot seven he was still stocky and wore his brown hair cut short in the military style. Cliff was a little taller, but he was skinny, so they might need him to crawl through the window. As Patrick neared the window, he was relieved to see that it was big enough for him to climb through easily.

The take-out window was sixteen inches high and two feet wide, a chute for passing out auto parts and accepting money in return. A metal plate on tracks could be slid down to close the window during the day when employees were working the counter inside. Also, a hinged door could be swung shut and locked.

Patrick felt his heart pumping, the adrenaline kicking in. His blue-green eyes moved from the window to the traffic on W Street.

Man, I am this far away from making it, Patrick thought as he walked toward the window. As soon as the words passed through his mind, they were replaced by another thought: *This is crazy. I can't believe I'm about to do this stupid junk. I'm about to rob this dude in the middle of W Street with all this traffic and I got one bullet in the gun.*

Every step toward the window spurred on the debate inside his head. *I'm this far from having a real life . . . I'm an idiot . . . No more madness, no more screaming and yelling, no more craziness . . . Here I am like a moron getting ready to rob this dude . . . I'm going into the Marines, I'm getting married . . . This is insane.*

At the window, Patrick stood face-to-face with Wells. Patrick tried to look calm, but inside he was antsy and anxious. *Don't spook the guy.*

He might pull a gun on you. Wells looked a little annoyed. It was almost closing time. He wasn't feeling well. He wanted to go home, and here's this kid . . .

"I want you to check to see if you have a clutch disc, pressure plate, and throw-out bearing for an '85 Nissan truck," Patrick said.

With his gloved hand, Patrick handed Wells a piece of paper with the part number that Archer had told him to write down. While he waited for Wells to look up the number, Patrick glanced over his shoulder at the cars driving by.

Patrick slipped off his right glove and laid it on the metal chute. His hand touched the gun in his pocket. He couldn't get a good look at Wells, who was off to the side, behind the hinged metal door. Even if he could see him, he wasn't sure what Wells looked like. All Robbie had told him was that the guy he wanted killed would be working alone that night.

Something about the boy at the window spooked Wells. He pretended to look up the part in a catalog, but all he wanted was for the kid to go away.

Wells handed the slip of paper back to Patrick. "I don't have it," he said. "I'll have to check tomorrow."

Patrick said he'd be back, turned, and walked quickly away. A surge of relief flooded over him. He felt he had been given a reprieve. He opened the door to Eddie's Mustang and slid into the passenger seat. He didn't want the other guys to see him scared. He didn't want them to think he chickened out.

"What happened? What's going on?" asked Cliff from the backseat.

"Everything's cool," Patrick replied. "We can do this tomorrow."

The Boys 1

Patrick Bonifay

I am sick of this shit, thought sixteen-year-old Patrick Bonifay as he rummaged through his sister's pill bottles in their mother's trailer. He had never been good at school, and now, early in the 1990–91 school year, he had been expelled from ninth grade at Escambia High for fighting.

Fighting, that's what he was good at. Since he was old enough to be shoved out the front door of the trailer, Patrick defined himself by his fists. In Brownsville, where the drug dealers, junkies, and prostitutes congregated in the trashy trailer parks along the railroad tracks, he had two choices—fight or stay inside. Staying inside was not an option. He didn't like the feeling of being confined, constricted, told to sit still and be quiet. He liked to move, run, play, fight.

Patrick had grown into a tough kid from a rough part of town. A part of Pensacola was refined, genteel, and proud of its past. Its

5

epicenter was Plaza Ferdinand VII in downtown, where the city originated in 1559. Mornings in the square began with the sun working its way down the thirty-foot obelisk monument to William Dudley Chipley, local hero of the Confederacy, lifting the dark veil of night off the bronze bust of General Andrew Jackson, who received Florida from Spain and raised the American flag on July 17, 1821, and giving a shine to the glossy black cannons from Spanish galleons aimed south at Escambia Bay. The part of Pensacola that revered the past, like few other places in Florida, had its own little Williamsburg-style Pensacola Village of houses, built in the 1800s, where people dress in colonial costumes.

But that wasn't Brownsville, where mornings began with hangovers, sore backs, and hypodermic needles left in the woods. Brownsville had been a white workingman's neighborhood of small frame houses and mobile-home parks of single-wide trailers when Mobile Highway was the main highway of the Florida Panhandle. The strong sense of community that existed in Brownsville began to erode with the construction in the 1960s of Interstate 10, which ran the length of north Florida and into Alabama, Mississippi, and Louisiana. Thirty years later, blue-collar Brownsville was down-and-out Brownsville. The remnants of its working-poor past were still there in the upholstery shops, car-repair businesses, and auto-parts stores, but the small brick businesses that once sold candy to children and the flat-roofed restaurants with the blue-plate specials of southern home cooking surrendered to thrift stores, pawn shops, and ethnic grocery stores. Respectable families moved out, and prostitutes, thugs, and drug dealers moved in. Those who remained in the early 1990s formed a community action group when prostitutes began to proposition men mowing their front lawns. The hookers didn't disappear; they just became a little more subtle. Cars pulled off Mobile Highway and trolled slowly down the side road that descended to the railroad tracks, past desperate, hopeful women who smiled and waved from a bus stop.

The tidy, tree-shaded trailer parks along Border Street slowly crumbled with time and neglect. Siding darkened with mildew. Floors sagged from wood rot. Leaky window air-conditioners were propped up by two-by-fours. Grass gave way to bare-dirt front yards. "No Trespassing" signs and skinny yard dogs too needy to bark at strangers protected the property and possessions of the poor.

Border Street was where Patrick's grandfather, James Scarbrough, had his truck-refrigeration repair business. Patrick and his mother, Theresa, lived in a trailer in the back of the business.

As soon as he was old enough for school, Patrick was in trouble. His teachers complained about him to his mother. Patrick doesn't pay attention. Patrick won't sit still. Patrick doesn't share. Patrick won't talk. Patrick walks into the classroom, crawls inside a cabinet, and spends all day there. Patrick fights with the other kids.

Patrick's mother took him to the doctors the school recommended. Your son is hyperactive. He has attention deficit disorder. He is emotionally disturbed. They prescribed Ritalin and placed him in classes for kids with emotional disabilities.

Theresa didn't tell the doctors, or the school, that Patrick complained about hearing voices after he started taking the Ritalin, so she stopped giving it to him. She didn't tell them, either, that when he was eleven or so he had told her that his biological father, James Bonifay, had molested him when he was eight or nine.

James and Theresa divorced when Patrick was two, and Theresa married Howard Crenshaw four years later. They moved into the two-bedroom trailer at the back of her father's business, next to the railroad tracks and close to the woods where the kids had to watch where they stepped to avoid the junkies' needles. Across the street, in a small frame house, a family of sisters prostituted themselves.

There were always more people in Patrick's trailer than there were places to sleep: Theresa, Howard, Patrick, Patrick's sister Jody, Jody's boyfriend, and anyone else who needed a place to stay until he found a better place to live. Sometimes Howard's cousin Robin Archer lived there. Even Patrick's father lived with them after his own trailer burned down. In Theresa's trailer, dinner was grab a plate and find a place to sit down. Wash your hands if you feel like it.

Patrick's mother understood the needs of her son and her failings as a mother. She had her own emotional problems, and a hyperactive, defiant kid was too much for her to handle. Her father agreed to let Patrick live with him in his modest, three-bedroom clapboard house close enough to the Pensacola Naval Air Station to watch the Blue Angels practice their maneuvers.

From the front yard of his grandfather's house, Patrick could see the jets in formation against the blue sky of the Panhandle and imagine himself inside the cockpit. A Marine Corps aviator, that's what he'd be.

Patrick loved his grandfather, and James Scarbrough loved him back. He saw something of himself in the boy. Scarbrough had grown up restless and rambunctious in Alabama, but he was an old-school disciplinarian. He knew what a boy like Patrick needed—structure, discipline, chores. Yard work was a good cure for a little Tasmanian devil like Patrick.

In his grandfather's house, Patrick washed his hands before he sat down to dinner and removed his plate when he was finished. He went to church every Sunday, whether he liked it or not. He had chores to do and a room to himself. It felt like a normal kid's house.

But there were problems in James Scarbrough's house as well. His second wife, Patrick's step-grandmother, didn't like having to raise someone else's child. Scarbrough felt, too, that Patrick ultimately belonged to his mother. So when he got the boy settled down, he'd send Patrick back to Theresa and the trailer in Brownsville.

Growing up in the limbo between his mother's trailer and his grandfather's house, Patrick lived inside the realm of the teenage mind ruled by impulse and fantasy. If he wanted something, he took it. If a friend suggested something, he did it. He was quick to anger, fast to fight. In his mind, anything was possible and everything was better than what he had. He imagined himself as a boy with many friends. He imagined himself a gangster. He imagined himself rich. In the supermarket, he gravitated toward magazines that displayed the wealth he expected one day would be his: exotic, expensive cars, big houses, fancy clothes. He devoured the military magazines, which fed his desire for adventure, bravery, and recognition. His imaginary life became so real, and his real life so dismal, that it became hard for him to distinguish between the two. Lies and truth were two sides of a double-sided coin.

Something inside Patrick liked the structure, restrictions, and discipline of his grandfather's house, and something else liked the freedom, looseness, and informality of his mother's trailer. He could no more choose which he preferred than his grandfather and his mother could settle on where he best belonged.

The day he swallowed his sister's pills, Patrick would belong to neither. He walked outside his mother's trailer and replayed the events that made him feel like suicide was his only solution. The boy whose jaw he broke, David Ramsey, was one of the preppies from Warrington whom Patrick detested. Nor did David care much for Patrick, the troublemaker from Brownsville who came to school wearing thrift-store T-shirts and acting like he was better than everyone else. The afternoon they got into it in the school parking lot, Patrick knocked David to the pavement and broke his jaw with a foot to the face.

Kicked out of school, Patrick was adrift at sixteen. He had fantasized about becoming a pilot, soaring high and far away from a miserable life of poverty, violence, and disappointment. Now, it seemed, he shot his own dreams out of the sky. He's inside this cockpit he can't escape, he's suffocating, spiraling downward, and there's no parachute, no escape. His mother seemed indifferent to his problems. His grandfather was pissed off and threatening to turn him over to the juvenile authorities.

Kelly Bland, Patrick's best friend and Cliff Barth's cousin, found Patrick outside the trailer, dopey on his sister's antidepressants. Bland dropped him off on his grandfather's doorstep. His grandfather thought Patrick was whacked out on drugs. They sat at the dinner table, neither saying a word to the other. When they finished eating, Scarbrough turned to his wife and told her to make sure Patrick was there when he got home from work the next day.

The next night, Scarbrough ripped into Patrick about drug use, getting kicked out of school, wasting his life, running with the wrong crowd, acting out of control. Things were going to change, he said. There would be a curfew, no leaving the house.

Patrick became frustrated. Every time he tried to explain that he wasn't high from drugs, his grandfather cut him off.

"Pop, you don't understand, man," Patrick said.

"I don't want to hear your excuses," his grandfather shot back. "I'm not going to tolerate you using drugs in my house."

The more his grandfather shouted, the more Patrick yelled back. He said he was going to move back to his mother's. He called his mother to come get him. A few minutes later, his stepfather arrived. As they were leaving, his grandfather was still getting on him.

"Man," Patrick said to Howard, "he's gonna make me break his jaw."

When they got back to the trailer, Scarbrough was on the phone to Theresa, furious with Patrick's parting threat. She handed the phone to Patrick.

"Don't go anywhere in the morning. I'm gonna take you and turn you over to the state," Scarbrough said.

"No you ain't," shouted Patrick, and hung up the phone.

Theresa and Howard watched as Patrick went back to his room and packed a duffel bag with a few shirts and some jeans. They listened as he dialed the phone and called a friend, Scott, to come pick him up on the street outside the trailer. He was running away from home, and they knew it. They let him leave without a word.

With his bag, Patrick walked down the street and waited. He waited for Scott to come take him away. He waited for his mother to come take him back. When Scott finally arrived, Patrick got in the car. That night, he slept on the floor of his friend's apartment. He spent another night sleeping under a bridge. The night after that, he fought a guy in the parking lot of a bar, men yelling and tossing cash on a car hood, and won enough money for a couple of nights in a motel. After that, he went to work for a drug dealer who employed a group of homeless teenagers to do whatever needed doing.

But life as a do-boy for a drug dealer wasn't the one Patrick had envisioned for himself. He still had ambitions to become a pilot, a military man like the other Bonifay men. One night on the back deck of a beach house owned by the drug dealer, Patrick sat smoking pot and drinking Mad Dog 20/20. He was looking at the stars when a plane flew overhead.

The distance between who he wanted to be and who he was had never felt greater. *Oh, man*, he thought, *I'm going to die out here. I don't want that.*

Toward the end of the summer of 1990, Eddie Fordham stole his father's ski boat. He was seventeen, about to enter his senior year at Escambia High, and there was this girl—a cheerleader with eyes so blue the boys called her Jewels—he wanted to impress. It was supposed to be just the two of them on his father's sixteen-foot Rankin bow rider, which he took without permission using a copy of the ignition key he had secretly made. But Jewels wanted to make it a party boat, not a romantic cruise, and invited along a girlfriend and three of the Brown Boyz, a gang of mostly Filipino and black kids who went to Escambia High.

Eddie eased his father's boat from the dock and piloted it to Bayou Texar off the Intracoastal Waterway, where he moored the boat. They started drinking beer as the sun went down on another muggy summer day. While the other guys were doing cannonballs off the deck and playing Marco Polo in the water, Eddie sat next to Jewels, close enough to smell the scent of the pomegranate-and-coconut shampoo in her hair. She had always treated him like a buddy, a bonfires-on-the-beach boy. He had something else in mind, and tonight, maybe tonight, was the chance to make it happen. Eddie leaned in to whisper something in her ear when the other girl, C.J., came stumbling from the bow, where she had finished off the last of the beer.

"Eddie Fordham," C.J. said, "I can see the words skinny-dipping written all over your face."

Eddie looked at her like she was a fortune teller dressed in denim cutoffs and a halter top.

"Naked," she said. "That's what you're thinking."

That was what he was thinking. Getting naked. If he got naked, maybe Jewels would too.

But before anyone got naked, one of the other guys, the one with a pierced nipple, discovered the empties rolling around in the bow.

"Red alert! All the beer's gone!"

Another guy popped his head out of the water on the pilot's side.

"Eddie, where in the world's all the beer?"

It's always my fault, Eddie thought. *It's my dad's boat, I bought the beer, I picked them up, but it's my fault there's no more beer.* No matter what he did—even stealing his father's boat—they still dismissed him as the rich kid, the spoiled momma's boy.

Eddie was his mother's miracle baby, her only child, born after the surgery to realign her uterus. He was named Larry Edwin Fordham Jr., after his father, but he was his mother's son—Eddie. He heard the legend of his birth over and over, how he was the first boy baby at the Huntsville, Alabama, hospital in so long that the doctors and nurses cheered his arrival. The lone blue-blanket baby in a nursery of pink-blanketed girls.

Maybe it started there, in infancy, this ease he had around girls and the difficulty he had making friends with other boys. He had what other guys envied—his own room in a two-story house overlooking a pool in the backyard; his own yellow 1965 Mustang; a closet full of designer clothes. And yet they never seemed to accept him.

Eddie's parents had grown up in Pensacola. In 1987 they moved to the older subdivision of Twin Oaks in the middle-class neighborhood of Warrington. They found a city not much different from the one they left in the 1970s. Pensacola missed the rapid population growth that had transformed much of the state into places that even natives barely recognized. Its beaches hadn't become a wall of high-rise condos. Its farms and fields hadn't become rippled seas of shingled rooftops. The city had much to offer—beautiful, unspoiled white-sand beaches, a past preserved in its historic buildings, and a strong cultural scene—but it lacked the desire to publicize itself as a tourist destination or a mecca for manufacturing and new business.

Because Pensacola had grown modestly, it never lost that small-town familiarity and "Old Florida" feel of its agrarian heritage. Larry and Diana moved back to a city that many of their friends, classmates, and relatives had never left. Unlike many other Florida cities, it wasn't hard to find people in Pensacola who were born there and never left, and others who moved away and later returned. In 1991, when the recession had stalled the city's population at fifty-eight thousand, 43 percent of Pensacola's residents were native-born Floridians, and another 33 percent came from the neighboring southern states. In the rest of the state, only 30 percent of the people were native Floridians and 16 percent were southerners by birth.

In Twin Oaks, where Larry and Diana bought a two-story colonial brick house on Schofield Drive, a shovel full of dirt could unearth the history of the place. Backyard bits of asphalt and concrete reminded residents that their subdivision was built on top of the original airstrips where the first Navy pilots were taught to fly. All their streets— Admiral Doyle, Rodgers, Cunningham, Billingsley, and Chevalier— were named for early pilots and naval officers.

For Eddie's parents, moving back to the place where they grew up and still had strong family ties, Pensacola provided a center of gravity that many Florida cities lacked. The past gave Pensacola a sense of permanence. But for Eddie, as an adolescent, there was no strong sense of belonging to anything or anyone. After three years in Pensacola, he still didn't fit in. He made the high school swim team, but he wasn't really anyone's teammate. He wasn't one of the stars, and those who were never asked him to join them when they were doing their guy things.

At eighteen, Eddie craved kicks and acceptance. He loved the adrenaline rush that came from rock climbing, rappelling down the side of a cliff, parasailing over the clear Gulf waters of Fort Walton Beach, racing the sailors from the Navy base in his high-performance, four-barrel Mustang. Oh, it felt so great pulling alongside those Navy boys at a traffic light, revving his engine next to them, the exchange of looks, a little smile on his lips. *Yeah, bring it on, guys. I'll race you light to light.*

But he could never find a group of kids who accepted him as one of their own. When he ran for student office and narrowly lost, it didn't make him feel less popular. It made him feel unpopular.

The teenage need to belong drew Eddie away from his middle-class life in Twin Oaks to the fringes of the Brown Boyz gang, whose crimes consisted mainly of home burglaries, car break-ins, and drug dealing. Eddie was never really one of them, but the Boyz let him hang around, and this gave Eddie some sense of being one of the guys and satisfied his need for thrills.

But on this night, next to Jewels on his father's boat, it was a different kind of thrill. As unsure as he was around other guys, Eddie felt cocky around girls, even those as beautiful as Jewels. His mind returned to the idea of skinny-dipping.

"You're sweating," Eddie said to Jewels.

"Girls don't sweat," she said. "We glisten."

"Then the bayou's just what you need to rinse all that glisten off," he said. "Come on, the water's great."

"No it's not," Jewels replied. "It's cold."

"I'll keep you warm," he said.

"Good try, Eddie."

But the slight blush on her face and the faint smile on her lips made Eddie think that if he just let the other guys get good and drunk, he might still have a chance of ending up alone with Jewels, undressing each other in the moonlight and making love in the water.

The beer didn't make the Brown Boyz pass out. It made them more reckless. With a boat full of empties, they swam over to a sailboat where they discovered a cooler of beer and a pair of water skis. One of them found a Jet Ski on the shore, and after several unsuccessful attempts to get it started they decided to tie it to the back of Eddie's boat and tow it. Stolen water skis, now a Jet Ski—this wasn't what Eddie had in mind for a night on the boat with Jewels.

"I don't remember asking anyone to bring back anything more than just beer," Eddie said.

One of the boys punched him in the arm: "Don't be a wuss, Eddie."

That shut him up.

Eddie was pushing the throttle of the boat as far as it would go, one of the guys bouncing on the seat of the Jet Ski, when the cops showed up. A beam from the spotlight on a patrol boat played over the water.

"Oh-oh," said the kid with the pierced nipple. "It's Eddie's mom. She found us."

"Don't say that," Jewels said.

"Gimme a break," he replied. "You've said it yourself—Eddie's a momma's boy."

There wasn't much time to debate Eddie's manhood as the spotlight settled on the group of kids standing on the deck of Larry Fordham Sr.'s boat. Eddie threw the boat into fast forward, but the Jet Ski acted as an anchor. One of the guys untied the rope, launching the boat into the air.

"Yee-haw!" yelled one of the guys, a beer bottle held aloft.

Eddie could feel the adrenaline kick in with the fear as he tried to outrun the patrol boat. It was just like the rush he got from racing the Navy guys stoplight to stoplight, only more intense—like being inside a video game instead of just playing it.

Eddie beat the patrol boat to the Hyde Park boat ramp, and everyone jumped into the water. The last Eddie heard from the pierced-nipple boy was, "Every kid for himself!" In his hands, the boy held the keys to Eddie's father's Chevy Blazer.

The last Eddie saw of him, the kid was behind the wheel of the SUV, C.J. by his side.

They left me! They shit on me!

The sick feeling of abandonment came with the adolescent understanding that his sense of acceptance was false, that his friends were not friends, that nobody really cared what happened to him.

In that same instant came another realization. The police were after him. Eddie started running.

Clifford Barth

George Wynne pulled the pickup behind the All Pro Sound car-stereo store on Beverly Parkway. It was late at night on December 22, 1990. The store was locked and dark. Clifford Barth climbed out of the truck along with Patrick Bonifay, Kelly Bland, and a kid named Eric. Cliff followed behind as they walked around to the front of the store. The whole time he was thinking, *I can't believe I'm doing this.*

It was a familiar feeling, this out-of-body disbelief. Cliff had felt adrift since he arrived in Pensacola in August ahead of his parents and sister. He was sixteen then and on his own for the first time, living with his aunt and uncle. The rest of the family was driving down from Alaska with a side trip to Ohio. His father, Walter, was a career Army man, and this transfer would be his last. His mother, Sheila, would be back with the family she left when she married Walt. She'd be home, one of the family again, and Walt would be near a military base that served the medical needs of old Army guys.

Cliff envisioned Pensacola as sun, beach, and girls, girls, girls. The Gulf of Mexico was nothing like the Gulf of Alaska. Pensacola was nothing like Anchorage. Pensacola had white-sand beaches and palm trees and girls in little bikinis. His first day on the sand of Pensacola Beach, beneath the summer Florida sun, he burned up like a slab of grouper on a grill.

But he liked Pensacola. It had a familiar feel. He wasn't living on an Army base like Fort Richardson in Alaska, but Pensacola was a military town. Even as it grew larger and more spread out, inching ever closer to rural areas like Beulah, where Cliff's parents had rented a house, Pensacola remained a company town where everybody knew someone who worked at the Naval Air Station or nearby Eglin Air Force Base. The military heritage of Pensacola, where the streets were named Navy Boulevard and Blue Angel Parkway, instilled a deep sense of patriotism that melded well with Deep South loyalties to God and country.

Loyalty to country didn't necessarily translate into loyalty to the federal government, though. Pensacola maintained that Old South resentment toward government intrusion on local affairs. A hundred years after the Civil War, Pensacola was still fighting for its independence against Washington, D.C. The city adopted the same posture toward the government that Alabama Governor George Wallace had taken, standing with arms crossed in opposition to federally ordered school desegregation. In the 1960s, an effort to preserve the undeveloped land on Santa Rosa Island as a national seashore park met with stiff opposition from those in Pensacola who didn't want the feds owning their beaches.

In its geography, history, and heritage, Pensacola was as southern as any city in Florida. It had never fully separated itself from the Old South. As a city, it felt closer to Alabama than to the rest of Florida. To the west is Mobile, to the north Montgomery. While on the opposite end of the state residents of Key West declared their independence from Florida by creating their own Conch Republic, Pensacolans periodically proposed their annexation to Alabama. Even Andrew Jackson, who lived in Pensacola for thirteen weeks as its provisional governor in 1821, acknowledged the city's emotional attachment to its northern neighbor in his parting toast: "Alabama, we love you, but we will not wed."

Generations of Pensacola high school graduates went to Auburn and the University of Alabama instead of Florida State and the

University of Florida, decorating their front porches with flags for Tigers and Crimson Tide instead of Seminoles and Gators. The New Orleans Saints, not the Jacksonville Jaguars, Tampa Bay Buccaneers, or Miami Dolphins, were the pro football team of Pensacola.

Pensacola's attachment to the rest of Florida has always been tenuous. Geographically, Pensacola is closer to Chicago than to Miami. Culturally and politically, it has more in common with Mobile than with Mickey Mouse. First established as a Spanish outpost, Pensacola has always maintained that outpost mentality. A sense of isolation pervades Pensacola, reinforced every time its residents look at a map of Florida and notice that their city missing. In the broad outline of the state, Florida seems to end at Tallahassee. On road maps, the Panhandle is often shown on a separate map from the rest of Florida, like a thumb severed from its hand.

If Pensacola is estranged from Florida, it holds a strong attraction as a magnet of opportunity and leisure for the rural masses from Alabama, Mississippi, and Louisiana who built ships, logged timber, and enjoyed the beaches with sand so white the dunes look like snowdrifts. Over its history, Pensacola has drawn Greeks, Norwegians, Spaniards, and Italians, but their influence has always been temporary or sublimated by southern culture, politics, and attitudes. Other port cities, such as New Orleans, became more liberal from the influence of imports and outsiders, but Pensacola's waters couldn't accommodate the big ships that conveyed people from different places with different ideas on things like race.

On the "Redneck Riviera," the Confederate flag flew with impunity. It took a boycott by black students, a riot, and a federal court order to get Escambia High School, an all-white school until 1969, to stop raising the Confederate flag during school events and playing "Dixie" at football games. It wasn't until the mid-1970s that the school's team changed its name from the "Rebels" to the "Gators."

If Pensacola was southern-fried conservative in its politics, it was rock-hard Bible Belt in its religious beliefs. The Southern Baptist heritage and Pentecostal influence gave birth to a virulent strain of right-to-life activists. An abortion opponent purchased land outside a women's clinic and erected a cemetery of fake tombstones to commemorate the lives lost to abortion. On Christmas Day in 1984, in a "gift to Jesus on his birthday," four young people bombed a Pensacola clinic and two doctors' offices. Pensacola was becoming a dangerous place to be an abortion provider.

In 1990, when Cliff's family moved to Pensacola, the Gulf War put the city's pride in God and country on full display. Pensacola bristled with patriotism. Sailors and airmen stationed in Pensacola were being deployed to fight Saddam Hussein in Iraq. Eddie Fordham's parents made the papers by surprising their neighbors with red-white-and-blue ribbons on their mailboxes when they awoke one morning.

As an Army brat, Cliff had moved around enough to feel comfortable in the role of the new kid in school. He made friends easily. But he hadn't found a group of friends yet, and that added to his feeling of detachment. Other kids saw Cliff as a headbanger stoner who had a wolf for a pet. Cliff didn't discourage the perception, but inside he had no clear idea who he was or where he was headed. He had no ambitions, no plans for what to do after high school.

It just felt easy to grab onto Kelly Bland. When Cliff first moved in with Uncle Johnny and Aunt Dianne, Kelly was living there, too. Bland was his mother's cousin, which made him Cliff's cousin, too. It felt good to have a cousin like Bland. He was older and big, built like a fullback. To Cliff, it was like inheriting a bodyguard.

Bland had a sidekick—Patrick Bonifay. Bland looked tough, but Patrick *was* tough. He acted tough, he sounded tough, telling all those stories about the fights he'd been in, how he knew martial arts. When Cliff first met him in that summer of 1990, Patrick had just returned to Pensacola from a juvenile facility in Mississippi. He had spent six months in boot camp for participating in a burglary of an auto-repair shop. Patrick bragged about it being a gladiator's school where he saw twelve fights in his first two days.

It was hard for Cliff to tell fact from fiction when it came to Patrick. Patrick was sixteen, just like Cliff, but he always had a plan, a scheme, or some crazy idea. To hear Patrick tell it, his life was like something out of a movie script, his own made-for-TV movie. He'd been in every strip club from Panama City to Mobile. He'd screwed a hundred women. He was the muscle man for a drug dealer, and man, he'd seen too many kilos of cocaine to count. He'd seen a coffee table covered end to end with cash. He once made one hundred dollars for beating up another dude in a fistfight in the parking lot of a bar.

Patrick was always coming up with these elaborate, far-out plans, always boasting about something that might or might not be true. Cliff could never tell which it was, so he stopped listening. When Patrick started his bullshit, in Cliff's head it was the static of a distant radio station.

So it always came as something of a surprise to Cliff when one of Patrick's schemes actually happened. One day Cliff went to the mall with Kelly and Patrick, and they walked into a jewelry store to try on pinkie rings and started talking about forming a gang in which every member would wear a pinkie ring. Another time, Patrick was talking about dropping through the roof of a pawn shop and stealing guns. Crazy stuff. But then the crazy stuff came true, and Cliff found himself crawling through the window of Audio Distributors behind Bland, Patrick, and this kid Eric, walking around, looking at stuff. Someone grabbed a home amplifier, and they walked out. Or following Patrick into a house on Burgess Road and walking out with some scuba gear and guns with Kelly waiting outside in his Camaro.

And now here he was again with Patrick, Bland, and Eric in front of the darkened front windows of All Pro Sound at a time when he should be at home in bed. Someone broke the window with a brick and unlocked the front door.

Once they were inside, Cliff felt like he was on one of those game shows where contestants try to load as much merchandise as they can into shopping carts in five minutes. Cliff and Eric headed to the display aisle with the car stereos. Bland and Patrick went straight for video equipment. They met at the rear of the store in a storeroom stocked with stereo equipment and speakers.

The back room had a set of double doors that opened to where George Wynne was waiting in the truck. It was Eric's job, as an expert kickboxer, to break down the doors. Eric took a couple of quick steps toward the door, jumped up, kicked the door . . . and bounced off. He tried it again, the Karate Kid, with the same result. Not even a dent. To Cliff, with time running out and the burglar alarm in his ears, it looked absurdly hilarious. He glanced at Patrick, Patrick looked at him, and without exchanging a word they charged the doors together, shoulders lowered. The doors flew open.

They ran to the truck, set down what they'd taken from the shelves, and ran back inside for the boxes of stereo equipment. Patrick said they needed to go, so everyone piled into the truck and Wynne took them down a dirt road and into some woods.

It was three days before Christmas, and in the back of the truck was $17,750 worth of stolen stereo equipment. A week later, Cliff turned seventeen. Three weeks later, he would be following Patrick through a window of Trout Auto Parts.

Trout Auto 2

The sense of relief that came over Patrick as he walked away from Daniel Wells at the window of Trout Auto on January 25, 1991, disappeared at eleven o'clock the next morning when Robin Lee Archer walked into Patrick's bedroom.

Archer was angry.

"You need to go back and finish the job," he yelled.

Patrick yelled right back.

"I ain't going to do it. I'm getting out. I'm going to be an officer in the Marines. I'm getting married. I ain't going to kill a man. It's not worth risking my life," he said.

Archer sneered.

"What life? You got nothing. You got no money. Your family's got no money. You're not going anywhere. You need the money, man."

"Dude, I know," Patrick replied.

Archer was the living, breathing embodiment of how miserable Patrick's life had become. Archer was a long-haired, scraggly bearded twenty-six-year-old with perfect implanted teeth he liked to show off. The teeth—and the white '85 Nissan pickup parked outside Patrick's trailer—were purchased with the insurance money Archer received from a motorcycle accident when he was twenty-one. The accident gave him things, but it also left him with nosebleeds and headaches, for which he took Demerol.

Except for the perfect teeth and spotless white truck, Archer was no better off than Patrick. He had no place of his own. He stayed with friends and relatives, moving from place to place as he moved from job to job. The best job he had was working as a counter clerk for Trout Auto Parts making $130 a week.

Trout Auto Parts was a family-owned chain struggling to compete against the national chains, the Pep Boys and AutoZones, by charging customers less. There used to be seven Trout Autos in Pensacola; now there were four. Employee turnover was high and wages were low. To supplement their pay, some of the employees stole car parts. Daniel Wells—twenty-five and making $5.75 an hour working the night shift nobody else wanted—would slip himself a twenty from the cash drawer and make it up by overcharging customers who ticked him off. Other employees, like Archer, made their money selling drugs. The late-night take-out window was their personal street corner.

Wells and Archer had attended high school together. They didn't get along then, and it was no different now. Archer was an indifferent, surly worker. He showed up late, if at all. Once he skipped work for three days without calling in. When he was there, he didn't like taking orders from Wells or anyone else.

Archer acted like he was the boss, not Wells. If Wells tried to show him how to do something, Archer would snap back, "You don't have to tell me. I know what I'm doing." But most of the time, he wouldn't. He wouldn't sweep the floors. He wouldn't stock the shelves. If he was behind the counter and someone needed help with a part, he treated the customer like an annoying inconvenience. In this business, up against the big boys, customer service was what mattered most at Trout Auto and what concerned Archer the least.

Wells didn't have the authority to fire Archer. Only Tim Eaton, Trout's general manager, could do that. Eaton's office was upstairs at the W Street store. He knew everyone who worked there and everything that went on. He knew that when Archer worked at the Ensley store, he brought a dog with him without asking anyone if it was alright. Not all the customers like dogs. You just can't have that, and now, at the W Street store, there was the indifference and the attitude.

If Archer acted like he didn't need the job, Eaton didn't need Archer either.

Archer didn't make a scene when Eaton fired him in March 1990. There wasn't any anger or threats. He even seemed a little cocky. He'd find another job, he told friends, easy. He always did.

He left, but he didn't go away. For all his boasting that he didn't need the place, Archer kept drifting back, hanging out with a couple of his Trout Auto buddies. He came by the W Street store one day, everyone standing around while Wells worked. The talk turned macho. Archer told Wells that he knew how to take care of his own problems. He asked Wells, "You want to know how?" Then he pulled back the front of his leather jacket and showed him the gun strapped to his chest. Wells didn't think much of it at the time. Just another loser trying to look tough.

Losing a menial, minimum-wage job didn't bother Archer. Losing a retail outlet for his weed and cocaine did. He needed money.

Inside Patrick's bedroom, Archer continued badgering Patrick to go back to Trout tonight and finish the job.

"You need the money. You know you do."

What Archer said was true. Patrick was poor, dirt poor, and so was his family. He was tired of having nothing. Tired of his sister coming home crying because the other kids teased her about the secondhand clothes she wore. Tired of having to break some preppie kid's jaw because he made fun of the dollar-store T-shirt Patrick was wearing. Tired, so tired, of feeling miserable.

I can do this, Patrick thought. *I've rolled people. I've broken into places. It's not that hard. I don't need to kill the guy. Just shoot him, get him down. Grab the money and get out.*

"Alright, alright already," Patrick snapped and walked out of the room, leaving Archer behind in his bedroom of the trailer on Border Street.

The Murder 3

On January 26, a Saturday afternoon, Eddie Fordham was working in the back of the Pensacola Navy commissary when the phone rang. It was close to five o'clock, almost quitting time. He picked up the receiver.

"I need you to come pick me up," Patrick said.

This had become the standard procedure. Patrick would call, Eddie would drive. In the three months since they first met, Eddie had become Patrick's personal chauffeur, his wheelman. Eddie drove Patrick on their double dates, to the mall, to drug deals where Pat exchanged stolen stereo equipment for drugs, or drugs for money. Eddie didn't mind. If you're a teenager, having wheels makes you cool, and Eddie wanted Patrick to like him. In some ways, Eddie envied Patrick, the kid who always seemed to have a joint in his pocket when they went to a party. Girls like that, a guy with weed, almost as much as they like a guy with a Mustang.

If it hadn't been for girls, Eddie and Patrick would never be in the same car together. Rachael, Patrick's girlfriend, had introduced Eddie to Nikki, her best friend. Rachael was a pretty, athletic, half-Filipina girl. Nikki was a blonde party girl who felt soft and warm in Eddie's arms. What started with Eddie picking up Patrick for a double date with Rachael and Nikki had become dial-an-Eddie whenever Patrick needed to be somewhere. It was getting old. Saturday was starting to feel like Friday night when Patrick called and asked Eddie for a ride, promising to buy the gas, and then having him drive all over the place until they ended up at Trout Auto.

"Aren't we meeting the girls tonight?" Eddie asked Patrick on the commissary phone.

"I talked to Nikki and Rachael and told them I needed you to drive me somewhere. They're cool," Patrick replied.

At home, Eddie got ready for his date with Nikki. He pulled on his black Z Cavaricci pants with the pleated waist and tight, tapered legs. He chose a white turtleneck and found shiny coins for his burgundy penny loafers. In the mirror, he examined his face. The girls thought he was cute. He was slim and tall, five foot ten. He had green eyes, thick reddish hair always neatly cut, and a boyish smile. Some girls thought he resembled the actor Neil Patrick Harris on *Doogie Howser, M.D.*

The phone in his bedroom rang sometime after seven. It was Patrick again.

"You got a ski mask?" Patrick asked.

"Sure I do," Eddie said. He still had his ski mask from when he lived in Charlotte. "What do you need a ski mask for?"

"I want to scare the girls," Patrick said.

Eddie was having problems with his Mustang. If he turned it off, it might not start again. He had taken to carrying two keys, leaving one in the ignition to keep the car running and using the other to lock the door. So Eddie was driving his father's Blazer when he pulled up to Patrick's trailer that night. Patrick came out wearing a long-sleeve checkered flannel shirt and jeans and carrying a blue bag with the handles of a pair of bolt cutters sticking out.

"Did you bring the ski mask?" Patrick asked.

"Yeah, I brought the ski mask," Eddie said. "You need bolt cutters to scare the hell out of Nikki and Rachael?"

"Naw, man, what's really going on is there's an old man out in Molina and he owes me some money," Patrick answered.

The old man kept his money in a strongbox beneath a sink in his house and they were going to rob the old man's house, Patrick explained. But first they needed to swing by and pick up Cliff. Eddie had met Cliff a couple of times, but he was Patrick's friend, not Eddie's. Cliff went to Tate High School, out in the sticks.

On the way to Cliff's, they were driving by a Kmart when Patrick asked Eddie how old he was.

"Eighteen," Eddie answered.

"Then you're old enough to buy bullets," Patrick said.

"What do you need bullets for?" Eddie asked.

"Cliff and I are going to do some target practicing at his place," Patrick said.

Eddie pulled into the Kmart. They walked inside and back to the sporting goods department, where the clerk told them he didn't have the .32-caliber shells they were looking for. Eddie asked how much a box of bullets was, and the clerk said fifteen dollars. Between the two of them, they didn't have enough. They'd have to get the rest from Cliff.

. . .

Cliff had woken up that morning with a tremendous sense of relief. *I'm not in jail.* The night before had been like a bad dream, and now he was fully awake, happy to be in his own bed. He lay in bed thinking of everything that might have gone wrong—what Patrick might have done with that gun, how close to disaster they had come. For whatever reason, Patrick had changed his mind when he walked up to that window at Trout Auto. And that was that. It was over. Whew. Close one.

Cliff spent the day doing chores, mostly picking up the dog poop from the yard and playing with Nishka, his wolf-and-husky mix. He had rescued her from a miserable existence chained outside some kid's house in Alaska. He had to pit his father against his mother to get to keep the dog. They already had a couple of other dogs, but Nishka was his. He groomed and fed her and entered her in contests where the winner was the dog that looked most like a wolf. That afternoon Cliff spent time with Nishka, running around in an old gold-and-brown checkered jacket and letting her chase him down until both the boy and the dog were too tired to play anymore.

Cliff was babysitting his sister Angie's little girl and watching TV when Patrick called early that evening. We're going back to rob Trout Auto, Patrick said. Cliff couldn't believe what he was hearing. He can't be serious. Not after last night. But the more Patrick talked, the more serious he sounded. Cliff tried to convince himself that this would just be a rerun of last night. Patrick wouldn't go through with it, he thought. He's not going to shoot anyone, and when it's over he'll get this crazy idea out of his head for good.

Cliff was watching his niece when Patrick and Eddie arrived. He gave them the money they needed to get the bullets. After they left, he took a shower. The water flowed down over his long, straight brown hair, over his thin lips, and off his chin. Cliff told himself he wasn't getting ready to commit a crime. He was just getting ready to go out. He always took a shower before he went out. He liked feeling clean.

Dressing for a night out, Cliff pulled on a pair of blue jeans and a black T-shirt.

Before Patrick and Eddie returned, Cliff smoked a little weed, just a hit or two, from the pipe he kept in his shirt pocket. He was half hoping that when they got back he could tell them he couldn't go because he had to watch the baby. That excuse evaporated when his mother came home just before Eddie and Patrick returned. He said good-bye to his mother, walked out the front door, and climbed into the backseat of the Blazer.

They didn't leave right away. In front of Cliff's house, Patrick loaded the bullets into the gun. He was fumbling with the bullets as he slipped them into the chambers of the gun. It was taking too long, and Cliff was getting nervous. *What if my mom walks out to see what we're doing out here?* And then another, more disturbing thought came to mind: *Why does Patrick need a fully loaded gun?*

The thought that they had a fully loaded gun nagged at Cliff on the way to Trout Auto. Friday night there was one bullet. The gun Kelly gave Patrick—the old long, blue-barreled .32-caliber Colt he stole from his aunt's dresser drawer—was empty, and Patrick had to pick through an assortment of bullets he kept lined up on a shelf in his bedroom to find one that fit the gun. One bullet. Tonight, many more. In the backseat beside Cliff was a blue book bag, the bolt cutters, and the ski mask he retrieved from the mailbox as they left his house.

Cliff rebutted the evidence of what was about to happen with the denial he kept repeating in his mind: *This is not happening. We are not going to do this. This is just one of Patrick's crazy ideas. He's not really going to do it. He's not going to shoot anybody. We're not really doing this.*

. . .

Seated beside Eddie in his father's Blazer, Patrick was determined to go ahead with a plan that never felt right. It should be George Wynne driving, not Eddie. Patrick called George his uncle, but he was the son of his grandfather's second wife, Mary. For a time, George and Patrick had lived together, slept in the same bedroom, in James Scarbrough's house on Navy Point. George was in his twenties, an ex-Marine. Patrick tried to model himself after George. He was going to join the Marines, just like George.

Yet on Friday night, outside a Junior Food Store in Beulah, when Patrick tried to persuade George to drive him to Trout Auto, George had flatly turned him down.

"Don't do this. It's crazy, it's stupid," he told Patrick. "If you get caught, you're going to do life."

"Don't worry about it," Patrick said. "Eddie said he'd do it if you didn't."

And instead of Kelly, Cliff was in the backseat. Kelly and Patrick were as close as two teenagers can get. They drank together, they fought together. They broke into houses and businesses together. Patrick saw in Kelly a reflection of himself: you see Kelly, you see me. Kelly was nineteen, bigger and tougher. He and Patrick were going into the Marines together in the buddy system.

Kelly had agreed to get Patrick a gun, but that was as far as he would go.

Patrick pushed aside the feeling that he was alone in this with two guys he hardly knew. He submerged his doubts inside the music blaring from the radio. Eddie and Patrick were always battling over what to listen to on the car stereo. Patrick dismissed Eddie's taste in music as "skating rink" music. Eddie didn't like Patrick's preference for rap, especially that new CD by N.W.A. and that song Patrick liked to listen to, "100 Miles and Runnin'."

A 100 miles and runnin', MC Ren, I hold the gun and
You want me to kill a motherfucker and it's done in
Since I'm stereotyped to kill and destruct
Is one of the main reasons I don't give a fuck.

Whatever Eddie had in the car stereo, Patrick wasn't listening. He was trying to talk himself into what he was about to do. *Get this crazy shit over. This ain't nothing. Get the money and go. Been there, done this. It's just another robbery.*

· · ·

Eddie sat behind the wheel of his father's Blazer parked across the street from Trout Auto Parts. He smoked a Marlboro Light. Next to him, Patrick was smoking a Kool. It was nearing midnight. The cigarette did nothing to calm Eddie down. This was like drag racing while sitting still. Eddie could almost taste the adrenaline. He felt like he was inside an episode of *Miami Vice*, casing the place.

Eddie was trying to look cool in front of Patrick. He didn't want to ask too many questions, seem too nervous or needy. He'd been puffing up macho for Patrick and Cliff. He wanted to prove he was one of the boys. He reminded them he'd been in trouble before. He'd been arrested. Whatever they were up for, he was down with it. Sitting there beside Patrick, watching Trout Auto, Eddie was thinking, *I'm in. I'm cool. I'm one of them.*

Eddie could see the clerk inside the store helping two customers. In the parking lot, a man was working on his car. The hood was up and he was bent over the engine. He finished and slammed down the hood. The clerk opened the door, let the last two customers out, and locked the door. They got inside a yellow station wagon and drove off.

"Let's go," Patrick said.

Eddie started the car and pulled across the street into the parking lot. He felt electric. Supercharged. Inside the excitement was a twinge of guilt and the knot of fear that came with knowing he was doing something wrong.

· · ·

Inside the store, Billy Wayne Coker was getting ready to count the cash and turn off the lights. Saturday was supposed to be his day off, but there was never really a day off. For most of his life, Coker, now thirty-five, had worked two jobs. And he was still poor. Before he landed the job with Trout for $4.95 an hour, he and his wife and their two kids had been living out of their car, and Wayne was bumming money behind University Mall to feed his family.

Wayne and Sandra Faye Coker were married on January 14, 1979, one month after they met. He was twenty-four. She was thirty. A year later their son, Christopher, was born, a hyperactive child with an IQ of 80. Their daughter, Michelle, was born the next year, around the time Sandra began to have panic attacks. She became afraid to drive the car. She stopped wanting to leave the house. Wayne, when he wasn't working, did the grocery shopping, took the clothes to the laundromat, and ferried the kids to school and doctor's appointments.

They lived in a narrow, two-bedroom rental trailer about a mile from the W Street store. In a few weeks, as the Cokers approached their twelfth wedding anniversary, Wayne would be eligible for one week of paid vacation. He needed the break and the money.

Buddy Turner, one of the managers, called Coker around 2:30 P.M. that Saturday to ask if Wayne could close up for Wells at the W Street store. Wells had called in sick, and Eddie Coffee could work part of the shift if Wayne could take over after closing the store at Ninth and Jordan.

Coker always needed the money, so he was happy to fill in for Dan. Wells was the one who trained him when he started working at Trout Auto just about a year ago. Coker's kids called him Uncle Dan.

Coker didn't bother to shave that day. His face, below his thick brown mustache, was stubble. He pulled on the green, short-sleeve shirt with the Trout Auto logo above his heart, a pair of white crew socks, gray slacks, and gray cowboy boots. Around his wrist he strapped a watch with a black plastic band.

Sandra and Wayne kissed before he left for work. At the door to the trailer, Coker paused and looked at his wife.

"Bye," he said. "I'll see you in a little while."

That night at work, Wayne smoked a cigarette and drank a can of Coke.

He didn't see the black Blazer pull into the parking lot with the three teenagers inside.

• • •

Eddie parked the Blazer a few spaces from the take-out window of the corrugated metal building. Patrick slid out of the passenger seat. He had Eddie's ski mask in one pocket, the gun in another.

As he walked toward the take-out window, Patrick felt pulled toward the window and held back by what he was about to do. Again, doubt competed with determination inside his head. *You're a jackass ... But I need this money ... You're not going to get away with this ... I can do it ... This is really stupid ... I'll shoot him in the butt, he'll fall down, I'll get through the window.*

At the window, just as he had the night before, Patrick asked the clerk for a car part. As he was asking for the part, the phone rang. When Coker reached for the receiver, Patrick reached for his gun. His back to Patrick, Coker looked over his shoulder. Patrick stuck the gun back into his shirt.

"I'll be right with you," Coker said, and turned his back to the window.

As Wayne turned away, Patrick thought, *This is it. Do it! Do it now!*

Patrick pulled the gun from his shirt and shot Coker once in the back. He heard him scream. The gunshot was so loud it left a ringing in Patrick's ears.

• • •

Inside the Blazer, the sound of the gunshot startled Cliff. He had been sitting in the backseat thinking this was just going to be a repeat of last night. Patrick would hustle up to the window, put on a little act of talking to the clerk, and hurry on back. *I wonder what his excuse is going to be this time,* Cliff thought, just before the gunshot shattered his delusions.

Cliff looked at Eddie with disbelief.

"He did it," he said. "The motherfucker actually did it."

Then Cliff turned his head to see Patrick standing by the window, waving his arms and shouting. He felt his heartbeat accelerate inside his chest and his hands begin to tremble. He was suddenly hot. His face was sweating. Like someone going into shock, his brain disengaged and his body took over. He grabbed the bolt cutters, the blue book bag, and his ski mask and climbed out the back door of the Blazer.

Cliff ran to the take-out window. Patrick was halfway through the window when he reached out his arm and shot Coker a second time, in the chest. Cliff started to follow Patrick through the window, holding the bolt cutters and book bag in his left hand, pulling himself through the chute with his right. He was halfway in before he realized he had forgotten to put his ski mask on. Cliff slipped back out the window, pulled his ski mask on. One of his gloves fell to the ground. He didn't bother to pick it up.

Back inside the window, Cliff felt his vision narrow as if he were crawling though a tunnel. Inside the store, he glanced at Coker on the floor and Patrick leaning over him. Then he focused on his job—cutting the locks. He knelt beside the padlocks on the safe beneath the counter. The bolt cutters he had carried through the window with one hand suddenly felt heavy in his hands. His arms were rubbery. He squeezed the jaws of the bolt cutters on the shackle of the lock, but nothing happened. He squeezed harder, but he couldn't cut the locks. He felt drained of strength.

"I can't cut the locks off, Pat!" he shouted.

"Give 'em to me!" Patrick yelled back and handed the gun to Cliff.

Cliff knelt beside Coker, but he kept his eyes on Patrick. Patrick snipped the locks on the safe and climbed clumsily onto the counter, stumbling in his hurry. He reached up with the bolt cutters to snip the two padlocks on the green strongbox where the cash and checks from the other stores were stuffed.

Cliff couldn't feel the gun in his bare right hand pointed at Coker. He couldn't look at Coker, but he couldn't block out his voice. Coker, shot in the back and the chest, never stopped talking. He was pleading for his life, not for himself but for his wife and children.

"Please, don't shoot me again," he begged. "I won't tell the police . . . Please don't kill me. I've got a wife and kids. My daughter is nine. My son is ten . . . Don't kill me. Please, don't kill me."

The sound of Coker's voice competed with the thought inside Cliff's head that they had screwed up, that it was a disaster.

"Pat, he's not dead," Cliff said.

Patrick jumped down from the counter and grabbed the gun back from Cliff.

Cliff jammed the money, checks, and envelopes into the book bag. In a hurry to get out of there, to get away as fast as he could from this nightmare of stupidity, Cliff was headed to the back of the store when he heard Coker say to Patrick, "Please don't kill me. I've got a wife. I got two kids."

"Shut the fuck up about your fucking wife and kids!" shouted Patrick.

In Patrick's mind, this had gone wrong from the very beginning. The big money Archer said was here, wasn't. Cliff was useless, couldn't even cut the damn locks. The guy had seen Cliff's face. Cliff had said his name. There was no getting out of this. Right here, right now, he could go to jail for life. This was armed robbery, this was attempted murder, this was . . .

Patrick held the gun to the left temple of Coker's head and pulled the trigger. He pulled it again.

• • •

Outside, Eddie was getting nervous. He had moved the Blazer from the front of the store to the dirt road on the side. *What is taking them so long? They should be done by now.* He was turning down the volume on the radio when the exit door exploded open and Cliff and Patrick came running out. They were almost falling over each other to get inside the car.

"Let's go! Let's go!" Patrick yelled.

"What?" said Eddie.

"Just go, man!" Patrick shouted.

Eddie gunned it and headed down the dirt road that ran next to Trout Auto and into a neighboring subdivision.

"Kill the lights," Patrick told Eddie, who turned off the headlights until they reached the subdivision.

Driving slowly through the residential streets, Eddie exited the subdivision and turned left on Airport Boulevard. As they neared a Motel 8, Patrick told Eddie to pull into the parking lot. There, in the backseat of the Blazer, Cliff counted out the money—some to Pat, some to Eddie, some to himself. Pat, Eddie, Cliff; Cliff, Eddie, Pat. When it was all divided up, Cliff and Patrick each got $700. Eddie's share was $665.

Pulling out of the parking lot and easing back onto Airport Boulevard, Eddie drove west toward Beulah to drop Cliff off at his parents' house. Police cars with their sirens screaming passed them, headed in the opposite direction.

Cliff thought about the phone dangling from the counter over the body of Billy Wayne Coker.

"There was a man on the phone, wasn't there, Pat?" Cliff said.

"Yeah, I think there was somebody on the phone," Patrick replied.

"You don't think they heard, do you?"

"Naw, man, don't worry about it."

On the way to Cliff's house, Eddie took a wrong turn on Kingsfield Road, where Patrick dumped the checks from the strongbox in a ditch alongside the road. After dropping Cliff off, Eddie got on Mobile Highway, heading back to Pensacola. It was almost 1 A.M., Eddie's curfew. There wasn't time to get Patrick to his mother's trailer in Brownsville and back to his house in Warrington.

"Why don't you spend the night at my place?" Eddie said to Patrick.

"Sure," Patrick replied.

When they got to Eddie's house, his parents were still out. The teens went upstairs to Eddie's bedroom. His room had French doors that opened onto a balcony overlooking the backyard pool. The room was big, as big as his parents' master bedroom just down the hall. The walls were a tropical blue and decorated with framed Budweiser spring break posters. Eddie slept in a nautical-style teakwood bed rimmed with ropes, a wooden ship's wheel on the wall above his headboard.

The bed matched Eddie's teakwood study desk. Eddie sat on his desk chair, facing Patrick on the bed.

"Do you want to know what happened tonight?" Patrick asked.

Eddie tried to act casual.

"Sure, Patrick, tell me."

"I killed a man."

"No, you didn't," Eddie said. "There you go again . . ."

"No, man, I'm for real," Patrick replied.

Then Patrick raised his foot so Eddie could see the blood soaked into his pants leg. Eddie looked at the blood on Patrick's pants, the blood that Patrick had brought into his house, his bedroom, and the thought came instantly into his mind: *That's the end of my life sitting right there telling me this ain't no joke.*

The Arrest 4

At 1 A.M., the phone beside the bed awoke Investigator Tom O'Neal. There had been a murder at Trout Auto Parts, and they needed him at the scene. O'Neal rolled out of bed and pulled on a pair of jeans, a shirt identifying him as from the Escambia County Sheriff's Department, and a pair of soft shoes.

O'Neal was one of four Escambia County homicide investigators. It was his turn on the murder rotation for the last week of January 1991.

An hour earlier, Jerry Walker had called the sheriff's department about something strange going on at Trout Auto Parts. A few minutes before midnight, Walker was in his mother's house, sitting on the couch, talking to a clerk at Trout Auto on W Street about the price for a carburetor. The clerk was quoting him a price when he screamed.

At first, Walker thought the clerk was playing a joke, just goofing off. Then he heard the clerk say "Get the hell out of here" before the phone was dropped. With the receiver dangling by its cord, the sound from the other end became muffled. Walker plugged a finger in his other ear so he could hear better what was going on inside the store.

He heard someone say "Fuck," and then, from a distance, he heard someone yell, "Hurry up and let's get the fuck out."

Then the phone went dead.

Walker didn't call 911. He grabbed a phone book and, flipping to the front, found the number for the Escambia County Sheriff's Department. Someone in the sheriff's radio room answered his call.

"Sheriff's communications," the person said.

"I was just, uh, on the phone with a guy from Trout Auto Parts," Walker said.

"Yeah."

"Talking to him on the phone."

"Uh-huh."

"And, uh, he was quoting me some prices and all of a sudden I heard a bunch of hollering and some cussing and stuff and then I didn't hear anything else. I didn't know, you know, exactly what was going on, so I figured, I figured I might call ya'll and see if you could check it out."

"What auto parts, which one was that?" the radio room operator said.

"I don't know," Walker replied. "It's in the phone book under the yellow pages. It's just got a number."

"Yeah, but there's a bunch of Trouts."

"It should be the only one that's in there," Walker said.

"What is the phone number?"

"Okay, hold on a minute and I'll give it to you."

"Okay," the operator replied, and then prattled on about how terrible the phones are at the sheriff's department, even the 911 phones, while Walker looked up the number.

"Let me find this thing, wait a minute," Walker said, and then read the operator the phone number. "I called back since then, you know, and it's just a recording saying their parts phones are busy, they'll be right with you."

"Yeah, right," the operator said. "Okay, we'll send somebody down there."

Seventeen minutes into Sunday, January 27, Escambia County deputy sheriffs Van Weeks and Carl Chapman pulled up to Trout Auto Parts at 5590 North W Street in separate cars. The front door was locked. The lights were still on. Weeks looked through the front window. On the floor, behind the counter, a man was facedown, blood spreading from his head like an open hand.

They found Billy Wayne Coker dead on the floor, the phone's receiver dangling from the counter, nestled between his knees.

• • •

By the time O'Neal arrived at Trout Auto at 1:30 A.M., half the department was already there. In the pulsating blue lights of a half-dozen patrol cars, nearly a dozen deputy sheriffs and officers were searching the crime scene behind the boundaries of yellow tape. The air was cool, the night cloudy.

O'Neal surveyed the crime scene. The business itself was a two-story building painted a worn-out green. It sat close to W Street with just enough room out front for a half-dozen parking spaces. The second-floor offices looked out on the busy street through narrow, horizontal windows. Above the front glass door, the red neon sign said "Open." Behind the glass door, a yellow sign proclaimed "Thanks for Trying Trout." Next to the door was a window with a metal chute.

O'Neal entered the building from the open side door and walked down the aisle to the front, where Coker's body lay on the floor behind the counter. The store was old and cluttered. Lists of phone numbers were taped to filing cabinets, their pages yellowed and curled. The computer terminal at the front counter also served as a bulletin board for sheets of paper taped to its sides. The keyboard, like the phone next to it, was stained with dirt and oil from men's fingertips.

The take-out window next to the front door protruded inside the store, a sheet-metal box about the size of an air-conditioning duct. On top of the metal chute was an odd assortment of items: coffee cups, a deck of cards, a portable radio, and a solitary spark plug. The metal door, hinged on the right side, was decorated with a rock station bumper sticker. Beside the window, a pair of jumper cables hung from a pegboard hook, dangling above a car battery.

Behind the counter, the EMTs had rolled Coker onto his back. O'Neal examined the body without touching it. Coker's hands were smeared with blood. Blood continued to pour from his head and was streaked in different shades like paint that had been spilled before it was stirred. Coker's shaggy brown hair swept over the left side of his face, partially obscuring his half-closed eyes. Below a thick mustache, his lips were closed in something that resembled a subtle smile.

Looking around the store, O'Neal could see obvious signs, among the open cash drawers dumped on the floor and severed padlocks, that somebody knew what he was doing. The green metal box, seven feet above the floor, had been broken into. Only someone familiar with Trout Auto would know that the box was a wall safe.

One of the officers showed O'Neal the evidence they had found in the fifty-five-gallon drum used for a trash can behind the counter: a pair of black leather gloves and a single black glove. Another officer introduced O'Neal to the store's manager, Timothy Eaton. Eaton had little to say except that Coker had not been scheduled to work that day. The night clerk, Daniel Wells, had called in sick, and Coker was filling in. Coker lived with his wife and kids in a single-wide just a mile south of the store. It was about 3 A.M. when O'Neal left Trout Auto to notify Sandra Coker of her husband's death.

• • •

Sandra was up, waiting for Wayne. She wasn't expecting the knock on the door. Lately she'd been having problems sleeping, but she always liked to be awake when he got home. The kids, Michelle and Christopher, were dozing in the living room after trying to stay awake so they could tell Dad about something exciting that happened that day.

Wayne should have been home a long time ago, Sandra thought. When he closed the W Street store he was always home by 12:20 A.M. or so, and it was 3 A.M. Normally, by now she would have been frantic, practically tearing her hair out with worry. But this night, for some reason, she felt a calmness, something like serenity. She thought maybe the computer at Trout was down again and Wayne couldn't finish his work. Maybe he was talking with someone on the phone and lost track of time. Lord, Wayne loved to talk. That was one of the things he was really good at: conversation. Sandra wasn't nervous, but she was praying, and maybe through the prayers came the calmness. A stout woman with long, dark hair and green eyes, Sandra prayed and paced inside the trailer.

The Cokers' trailer was easy to find: it was the first one on the left in the small trailer park off W Street. The knock startled her. When she opened the door, she saw O'Neal and victim's advocate Mary Rebber standing outside. She didn't know Rebber, and it didn't register in her mind that the man dressed in a leather jacket with a fur collar and insignia was with the Escambia County Sheriff's Department.

She didn't think to ask who they were or if they wanted to come inside, but she came right out with the first thought in her mind.

"I know this must be about my husband, because he's too late getting home from work," Sandra said.

"May we come in?" Rebber asked.

"Oh, I'm sorry," Sandra replied. "Please come in."

Inside the trailer, there was an awkwardness as the three adults stood together and the children slept—Michelle in a rocking chair and Christopher on the couch.

"Mrs. Coker," Rebber said, "can we get you to sit down?"

Sandra pulled Wayne's chair out from the dinette table and sat down. Rebber sat at the table with her. Sandra kept waiting for her to say something, but Rebber seemed to be searching for the right words and failing to find them. Sandra studied Rebber's face, intent on the other woman's large brown eyes, as if trying to read her mind.

"So this is about my husband?" Sandra asked.

"There's been an accident," Rebber replied.

In Sandra's mind, the word "accident" formed around the idea of Wayne driving too fast and being in a car crash. Maybe he's still alive, she thought.

"Is Wayne okay?"

Rebber hesitated.

"No," she said.

Sandra stared at Rebber.

"Is Wayne dead?"

"Yes."

"No, that can't be. He was just here," Sandra said, shaking her head. "He was just here a few minutes ago."

Wayne had been home for a sandwich and a Pepsi after closing the Ninth Avenue store and taking over at W Street. But that had been hours ago.

"Mrs. Coker," Rebber said, "yes, Wayne is dead."

Sandra cried out, fainted, and fell to the floor. When Rebber and

O'Neal revived her, she returned to consciousness with an odd feeling of timelessness. All sounds were gone. She couldn't hear or feel herself breathing. There had been an accident. Wayne was dead. The world had stopped.

"Don't tell me how it happened. Don't tell me anything," Sandra told Rebber and O'Neal.

"Is there someone we can call?" O'Neal asked.

"Call my mother," Sandra said, and then instantly took it back. The news could give her mother a heart attack. "No, don't call my mother. Call my sister."

"We're going to have to tell the kids," Rebber said.

"No!" Sandra said. "Don't tell the kids. They love their daddy too much."

But the children were now awake, and they knew that something was wrong and that it involved their father.

"Momma, where's Daddy at? Where's my dad?" Christopher asked.

"Momma, is Daddy gone? Is Daddy gone?" Michelle said.

While Sandra and Rebber tried to calm the children, O'Neal stepped outside the trailer to call Sandra's family in Milton, about twenty-five miles from Pensacola, and also a minister whose card Sandra had handed him.

They all seemed to arrive at the same time. The narrow little trailer was crowded with Sandra, her father, brother, sister, the two kids, Rebber, O'Neal, and the minister. Everyone in the trailer heard one word of O'Neal's conversation with the pastor: "Gunshot."

Sandra turned to Rebber. "Mary, gunshot? Wayne was shot?"

"Mrs. Coker, there was a robbery tonight. They went in and Wayne was killed," Rebber answered, trying to keep Sandra calm as the children began screaming.

In Sandra's mind, the new reality of this timeless world began to take shape. The future was gone. There was no more thought of looking for a new place to live or planning that one week of vacation Wayne had coming at the end of the month. The past—their years of marriage, their struggles with poverty, the strange sense of creepiness Wayne felt when he worked the W Street store—was irrelevant.

My gosh, Sandra thought, *this is just horrible. Wayne is dead. He's been shot. Nothing is the same.*

It was 5 A.M. when O'Neal returned home. His wife knew better than to ask. From the moment he entered law enforcement, O'Neal cleaved his life in half. Work was work. Home was home. He shaved, showered, ate something, and drove to the office.

O'Neal was thirty-two-years old. Standing about five foot eight, he had a trim build, a full mustache, and reddish hair. He'd grown up an Army brat, living on bases across the country, but he graduated from Pensacola's Washington High School in 1976. His father had joined the Escambia County Sheriff's Department as a patrol officer after his retirement from the military. In 1981, after a few years working in retail and a few more in the Florida Highway Patrol, Tom followed his father into the sheriff's department. Seven years later, he became a homicide investigator. Trout Auto was his first chance, in three years in homicide, to lead a major murder investigation.

O'Neal began with a logical suspect. Wells had worked at Trout for a couple of years, left for another job, and had been back at Trout for about a year. He was the store's co-manager, but it wasn't hard to advance at Trout Auto. In the past year, fifteen employees had come and gone. Wells dreamed of leaving, too, maybe getting a job with Orkin Pest Control for $8.50 an hour.

O'Neal interviewed Wells that day and asked if he was willing to take a lie-detector test. Wells agreed. Three days after the murder, he sat down for the test. He was nervous and emotional. Before the test started, he choked up while talking about Coker's children. He asked the polygraph examiner what if, for some reason, the test showed he had lied: Was he going to be arrested and sent to jail?

He started crying.

"I feel guilty. I'm trying to be honest," he said. "Wayne died for $4.95 an hour. I only make $5.75 an hour. What scares me is I would have been there if I hadn't called in sick. They didn't have to do it to Wayne. He didn't have anything to start out with."

Then Wells told them who he thought was responsible: Robin Archer. Archer blamed Wayne for getting him fired in March. If someone inside Trout had set this up, Wells said, it was probably Robbie.

Wells then reiterated what he had told O'Neal about the night before the murder when someone approached the parts window just before midnight. Something about the guy, some kid, spooked him. He was wearing a long coat and gloves, and was constantly glancing over his shoulder as if he were looking to see if anyone was around. Wells said he felt relieved when the guy walked away. As soon as the kid left, Wells closed the metal door and secured it with a screwdriver. He turned off all the lights and stood in the darkness shaking. He'd been robbed once before, around Christmas 1989, by two guys with a sawed-off shotgun. They forced him to lie facedown on the floor while they opened the cash register and stole merchandise. He never got over the experience. It stayed inside him like a virus.

Wells had thought about calling the police the night of January 25, but he didn't. If he had, he said, he might have saved Coker's life.

Wells ended by insisting again that he did not kill Coker, had never planned with anyone else to kill Wayne, and didn't know for sure who killed him.

The polygraph did not completely exonerate Wells. The examiner noted his body language—how Wells crossed his arms and kept them crossed when answering questions about the murder but not when he was answering other questions. The test also showed some degree of deception when he was asked two questions: "Regarding Wayne's death, are you deliberately withholding any information about it?" and "Did you know about the robbery before it happened?"

O'Neal ordered a criminal background check on Wells. It came back with arrests for battery on a police officer, speeding, and DUI. O'Neal was also hearing rumors of drug dealing at Trout Auto involving Archer and the possibility that Wells was involved. He learned from the narcotics division that dealers inside Trout Auto were using the after-hours take-out window to supply their clients. He also heard rumors that Wells might have shorted one of Archer's dealers some money. If so, Wells had had reason to be spooked that night.

• • •

In the bedroom closet of Eddie Fordham's room hung the winter-style Body Glove wet suit with full arms and legs he had bought with the money from Trout Auto after the murder. That Sunday, Eddie, Nikki, Patrick, and Rachael had gone to the Cordova Mall together. The girls could tell something was wrong. The boys were more subdued than usual, and evasive about where they'd been and what they'd been doing last night. It was the last time the four of them would be together, walking through the mall.

Eddie bought his wet suit. Patrick was spending money too, buying Rachael a brown leather jacket with green shoulders and a dainty ring with a blue sapphire stone and two tiny diamonds for seventy-five dollars. Rachael thought of it as something like a promise ring. He thought of it as more like an engagement ring. Patrick and Rachael had talked about their future together. He had told her he knew a way to get $50,000, enough money for them to be happy together forever.

Eddie wore the wet suit once, waterskiing off Navy Point, but mostly it stayed in his closet out of sight, like the memory of the murder in the back of his mind. He concentrated instead on graduating from Escambia High. He needed one more credit, an English class, and he'd be out of high school and into the Navy, where he hoped to join the SEALs as a search-and-rescue diver. He became part of Project Graduation, helping to plan the ceremonies and parties. He auditioned as the narrator for a video yearbook, and was chosen as the voice of Escambia High School, Class of '91.

Patrick was still calling Eddie for rides, and sometimes Eddie agreed, just to keep things cool between the two, but often he would make up an excuse: I can't, it's a school night, my parents want me to stay home. In avoiding Patrick, Eddie spent more time with Nikki, who was teaching him how to drive a stick shift.

In early February, Eddie took Nikki out to dinner at Marcelli's Italian Restaurant, where his great-aunt had once lived upstairs when it was a pizza shop owned by his mother's side of the family. Eddie had a surprise for Nikki: a gold tennis bracelet he had bought for sixty dollars with the idea of giving it to her as a Valentine's Day present. But he was thinking maybe tonight, over a plate of spaghetti sauce passed down from his family, was the right time. Why wait? When Nikki wasn't around, he showed the bracelet to the maître d', a friend of the family, and asked Franco what he should do.

"You should give it to her now," Franco replied, "because we are never promised tomorrow."

• • •

In the days after the murder, Patrick was emotional and weepy one minute, cold and distant the next. He confided in Jody, telling his sister what he had done.

"Do you still love me?" he asked.

"Yes," she said, "but what you have done is so stupid, so, so, stupid."

When his mother left for work, Patrick stayed in bed crying. When she came home, she knew something was wrong.

"What's going on?" Theresa asked him.

"What if you've done something horrible?" he said.

"What?" she asked. "What have you done?"

And then the tears stopped, and his face went blank.

"Nothing. Forget it."

Patrick never told her what happened that night. He gave her money, but he never said where it came from. She was afraid to ask, and even more scared to know.

Patrick was at war with himself. One minute he thought about turning himself in, and the next he got so scared that Eddie was going to tell someone that he asked Kelly to put some fear inside of Eddie. He thought about Rachael, and the ring he'd given her. He's not going to jail, he's getting married. He needed to stop thinking about what happened that night. He needed to focus on getting that night school GED so he could join the Marines with Kelly.

A few days—maybe a week—after the murder, Rachael and Patrick went to Johnson's Beach to watch the sunset. The beach was one of their favorite places when they weren't at the Motel 6 on Highway 29, smoking, drinking, and having sex. Rachael knew Patrick was one of the bad kids, and in some ways that was what she found attractive about him. But what kept her with Patrick was another side of him— the funny, attentive, doting, sweet-voiced Patrick who treated her like royalty. Whatever she wanted to do, they did it. He was all about her, and she loved that about him.

It was cool that night on the beach, and as the sun went down it began to turn colder. Rachael wore the leather jacket Patrick bought her. She had his ring on her finger. Patrick had on a thin shirt. All he could think about was how cold it was and how he wished he had worn a jacket himself. Rachael looked beautiful. Patrick was freezing.

In the days after the murder, Cliff was trying to act like nothing had happened, nothing had changed, nobody had died. It wasn't working. He went to school, but he couldn't concentrate on what the teacher was saying. He came home and played with his dog, but it wasn't fun anymore. He rode his four-wheeler into the woods by the pond and got high, but the pot didn't relieve the stress. He smoked more dope more often, but it always had the opposite effect of what he intended. It didn't help him relax and forget; it made him more nervous and paranoid. The murder was always there, in the front of his mind, on top of everything else.

A few days after Coker's death, Cliff rode the school bus to Tate High. In the afternoon, when he stepped off the bus a few blocks from his home, an Escambia County deputy sheriff's car was behind the bus. Cliff wasn't surprised to see the patrol car. He knew the deputy lived a few doors down from his house. But having to walk past that car, forcing himself to look casual, making himself raise his hand and acknowledge the deputy, freaked him out.

At the front door of his house, Cliff paused and looked toward the patrol car, waiting for it to pull around the bus and into his driveway. He walked through the door and into his bedroom, where he sat sweating, his heart pounding. *Was he waiting for me at the bus stop? Was he looking at me differently? Did I look normal when I walked by? How long will it take before I get caught?*

⋯

Coker's murder had Pensacola on edge. In the days leading up to the murder there had been thirty-one robberies in Escambia County. Coker was the third clerk killed within a week. The day before the murder, a fifty-year-old night clerk at a Fort Walton Beach motel was shot and killed. A few days before that, a fifty-nine-year-old pawn shop employee was robbed and killed. Police assured the public that the wave of murders was just a coincidence, but clerks and store owners began taking additional precautions to protect themselves.

Pensacola was no stranger to high-profile murders and notorious killers. Ted Bundy, on his way out of Florida after killing two sorority sisters in Tallahassee, was stopped on W Street in Brownsville in the early hours of February 15, 1978, after a Pensacola police officer checked the license plate on Bundy's VW Beetle and found it had been stolen.

In 1983 the owner of a beauty shop in Gulf Breeze was arrested for trying to kill her fiancé with a bomb that exploded beneath his car on the corner of Garden and Baylen Streets in downtown Pensacola. When police delved deeper into Judy Buenoano's past, they connected her to the poisoning death of her first husband in 1971, the drowning of her mentally disabled son in 1980, and the suspicious deaths of two other men with whom she had had relationships. Dubbed the Black Widow, Buenoano was sentenced in 1985 to die in the electric chair.

In 1989, Timothy Robinson joined Judy on death row. On August 18, 1988, Robinson, Michael Coleman, Bruce Frazier, and Darrell Frazier—all members of a drug gang known as the Miami Boys—had forced their way into a home looking for drugs and money that had been stolen from them. They ended up sexually assaulting, torturing, and killing Mildred Jean Baker, Derek Devan Hill, Michael Alfonso Douglass, and Michael Anthony McCormack.

Three years later, police were looking for Coker's killer. Shortly after the murder, Wells gave a description of the person he saw that Friday night to a deputy sheriff who drew a sketch. The drawing appeared in the *Pensacola News Journal* and on local TV stations a week after the murder. The person in the sketch looked a lot like Cliff.

The sheriff's department also released to the press the description of the two men seen on the store's black-and-white surveillance video. The tape skipped back and forth between the front of the store and the warehouse in the back. It showed two young men inside the store, both wearing ski masks. One had on a checkered long-sleeve shirt; the other wore a black T-shirt. With the sketch and the videos, O'Neal believed he was looking for white males in their twenties. It never occurred to him that the killer was a high school student.

Tips started coming in. On O'Neal's desk in the middle of the second-floor bullpen of fifty officers, the pink message slips began to stack up. A woman called about a young man in his twenties, maybe thirties, who got defensive and whose voice got real high when he talked about Trout Auto. Another person left a message about a customer, a white male, five foot eleven, who came into her store acting strangely. He matched the picture in the *News Journal*. A reporter with Channel 10 called about a viewer who said she knew the man in the sketch. There was a message from Sandra Coker, and another from Jerry Walker, the man who was talking with Wayne on the phone when he was being shot.

In a stack of files, O'Neal had a list of seventeen suspects, nine of whom were in prison or jail. The Department of Corrections sent a printout of forty-three men convicted of robbery who had been released from prison since April 1990. O'Neal was working slowly through the names of twenty-seven men who matched the description Wells gave them. On another printout he had every current and former employee of Trout Auto.

Since the murder, O'Neal had been spending sixty or seventy hours a week on Trout Auto along with two other investigators, Tom Martin and Allan Cotton. They were working hard and getting nowhere. They had no solid leads, and one possible suspect who seemed less suspicious all the time.

Then Jennifer Tatum Morris called.

· · ·

Recently divorced, Jennifer Morris had started dating Kelly Bland. About two weeks after the murder, on a Tuesday, Patrick called Morris and asked her if she could give him a ride after his night class at Escambia High.

"Jennifer," he said, "I need to talk to you."

"Okay," she said. She had a class at Pensacola Junior College until 9 P.M., and she would pick him up after class. Morris pulled up to Escambia High around 9:15, picked up Patrick, and stopped at the Albertson's for some groceries on the way back to her place. On the ride there, Patrick had little to say.

When they got to Morris's apartment, she started putting away her groceries. Patrick flopped down on the loveseat.

"Well, what do you need to talk to me about?" she asked.

"I did something kind of, you know, kind of wrong, and I don't want Rachael to find out," he said.

"What did you do?"

"Did you hear about that Trout murder?"

Morris said no, she hadn't heard anything about it.

"Well, I did it," Patrick said.

"No, you didn't. You didn't do that," Morris said.

But when Patrick said yes he did, she asked him why. Because he saw my face, Patrick said. I was robbing the place, and he saw my face, and I killed him.

"Well, what are you going to do?" Morris asked.

"Nothing."

Morris drove Patrick home that night. Three days later, she called the police.

• • •

On February 11, sixteen days after the murder, Morris sat down with O'Neal in an office at the sheriff's department and told him what she knew. Eddie and Patrick had shown up at her house the Friday night before the murder looking for Kelly Bland. She overheard Kelly and Patrick talking about a gun. The next night, Eddie drove the car. Patrick killed the clerk at Trout while he was begging for his life. A former employee helped him set it up. Some guy named Cliff was part of it, too.

"He killed him because the man saw his face," Morris told O'Neal.

For the first time, O'Neal knew who he was after: a kid. A kid capable of murder without mercy.

The next person O'Neal needed to talk to was Kelly. At 3:30 that afternoon, he sat in the same chair that Jennifer had sat in earlier.

Kelly told O'Neal, Martin, and Cotton that Patrick got the gun from him on Friday, returned it on Sunday, and told him to get rid of it. A couple of days later, Patrick told Bland what had happened.

"He shot the guy," Kelly said. "He went through the window. The guy was telling, you know, 'I got kids, I got a wife.' And then he shot the guy again, and then they got the money and then as he was leaving, he shot the guy four more times in the head. The next day, or two days later, he gave me the gun and that's when I got rid of it."

"Did he tell you who was with him?" O'Neal asked.

"Yeah, he said, uh, Eddie Fordham and Cliff Barton," Kelly said, giving O'Neal a wrong name for his cousin.

The interview with Kelly lasted five minutes. O'Neal knew who the killer was, who the driver was, who the accomplice was, and who set it up. He needed to act fast.

. . .

At 4:30 P.M., O'Neal and Martin pulled into the parking lot of the Naval Exchange Commissary at Corry Field. On the way over, Martin told O'Neal that he knew Eddie. They both lived in Twin Oaks. Eddie mowed Martin's lawn. Martin knew Eddie's parents, Larry and Diana. Eddie had been in trouble before, Martin told O'Neal, and Larry had always been there to bail him out.

Eddie was working the deli counter, as he did every weekday afternoon. An average student, Eddie got out of school early as part of Escambia High's diversified cooperative training program—a work-study program for potential dropouts, his assistant principal called it. He'd been at the part-time job for about a year, earning forty-five cents an hour less than Coker.

The commissary door opened, and Eddie looked up to see two men dressed in sport coats and slacks. They asked him if that was his yellow Mustang parked outside. Eddie recognized one of the men as his neighbor, Mr. Martin. The other man told Eddie they needed to talk to him and asked him to step outside. As Eddie took off his apron, the other officer added, "You better clock out."

. . .

Eddie was not surprised to see the two plainclothes officers. He had recently been contacted by another deputy sheriff about a Brown Boyz burglary, and he was thinking that that was what O'Neal and Martin wanted to talk about. As they walked past his car, they asked if it was locked and secure. As soon as he said yes, Eddie felt himself being pushed up against a police car and having his hands cuffed behind his back. O'Neal told Eddie he was under arrest for the Trout Auto Parts murder and read him his Miranda rights.

Eddie wasn't thinking about his rights. He was thinking about his father. His father had always been there before when he'd been picked up. His would want to be here with him. He'd get him a lawyer.

"Where's my father?" Eddie asked.

Neither man answered. O'Neal opened the back door and slid Eddie inside.

From the backseat, Eddie was starting to panic, tears in his eyes, when Martin turned toward him with a calm and reassuring voice.

"Look, Eddie, we know that you're the least involved in this matter. That's why we picked you up first. You were just driving. You see, we already know what happened. Son, you were in the wrong place at the wrong time. You've made some wrongs, Eddie. I'm giving you a chance to make some rights."

Eddie felt a little better. He started to talk, his voice full of emotion, but Martin interrupted him.

"Wait until we get to the office."

At the sheriff's department, Eddie was led upstairs to a large, open room filled with deputies and surrounded by six glass offices. He'd been there before. He knew the drill—talk to the cops, get turned over to juvenile, call his father to come pick him up. But he wasn't eighteen then. Legally, Eddie was now an adult. O'Neal was under no obligation to notify his parents of his arrest, but he also knew he was dealing with a teenager. He didn't want to take Eddie into an inter-rogation room, where the kid might get scared and refuse to talk. So he led Eddie, followed by Martin and Cotton, into one of the glass offices. O'Neal wanted Eddie in a place that was comfortable, a homey office with a desk, filing cabinets, a couple of chairs, and the personal belongings of a man's life. The stark interrogation room normally used for questioning a suspect was for intimidation, and O'Neal wanted cooperation.

Eddie felt relieved when they unlocked the handcuffs, but as soon as they sat him in a chair in front of the desk they locked one of his wrists to the arm of the chair. For a moment, it was just Eddie and Martin in the room.

"You want to call your parents?" Martin asked.

"No," Eddie replied. "I want to know exactly what's going on before I call them."

Martin nodded and left the room.

O'Neal came in, and from the moment he saw him, Eddie didn't like him. O'Neal was young, much younger than Martin, and he came across as a tough, gung-ho cop with an attitude.

"I want to make that phone call," Eddie told O'Neal. "I want to call my mom and dad. I want to call them now."

"Have you ever been to jail before?" O'Neal replied.

"Yeah, I've been on jail tour," Eddie said.

"What I mean is the big house," O'Neal said.

O'Neal looked cocky to Eddie—smug and confident, like a gambler who knows what cards you're holding. An uneasy feeling began creeping into Eddie's gut that this was already out of control, that it was beyond anything he could handle himself. O'Neal was talking, but all Eddie could hear was the panic inside his head: *Where's my dad? I need my dad!*

. . .

To O'Neal, Eddie looked like one of those kids who think the juvenile justice system is a joke. Actions without consequences. Crime without punishment. He can ask to call his mommy and daddy all he wants, but he's not a kid anymore. He's eighteen. He's an adult now. That's why they picked him up first—legally, he's an adult. Keep the parents out of it.

O'Neal pulled a chair up next to Eddie, just close enough to create a zone of comfort but not so close as to be intimidating. Martin sat in the chair on the other side of the desk, and Cotton took a seat by the glass wall of the office.

Before the questioning began, O'Neal read Eddie his Miranda rights again. Then he asked Eddie to sign a waiver agreeing to talk with them without a lawyer present.

Eddie hesitated. Martin came over to place a hand on his shoulder.

"I know this is going to be rough on you, but Eddie, son, we need you to help us get Patrick Bonifay. Think—what would your dad do if he was in your shoes?"

"He would probably try to help," Eddie replied.

"Then make your father proud and do what he would expect you to do," Martin said.

All they want to know, O'Neal added, is what happened that night.

They questioned Eddie for about a half hour about the events of Friday night and Saturday, a dress rehearsal for the moment they turned on the tape recorder and created a permanent record of Eddie's version of what happened at Trout Auto.

"What was the purpose of going to Trout that night to start with?" asked O'Neal.

"They just told me to drive up to Trout and that Pat had to check on some things. So I drove up to Trout and I parked on the side of the parking lot and he got out of the car and had a conversation with the man and came back to the car," Eddie answered. "They were talking about you know everything's alright, it's cool, we can do this tomorrow night, you know. We can do this or something the next night. I don't remember exactly how I got up with Pat, but we got together and he asked me to bring a ski mask with me and I said alright, so I brought a ski mask with me."

When Eddie mentioned the ski mask, O'Neal asked him what it looked like. Eddie's description of the mask matched what O'Neal had seen on the surveillance tape.

Eddie told O'Neal about driving to Kmart to buy some ammunition, but the store didn't have the right kind. So he drove to Cliff's house, but Cliff wasn't ready. They left Cliff's house and drove to a Wal-Mart to buy the bullets. O'Neal could feel the pieces snapping into place. Now he knew who supplied the ski mask in the surveillance tape and where the bullets came from.

"And then we went back to Cliff's house and then Cliff got in the truck and he had a ski mask and I knew then that there was going to be a burglary. I knew then that there was going to be a burglary and this was, oh, about forty-five minutes before it all happened," Eddie said.

On the way to Trout that Saturday night, Eddie said, Patrick talked about what he wanted Eddie and Cliff to do. Patrick would go to the window, Eddie and Cliff could keep an eye on the traffic, and when he was ready, he'd signal for Cliff.

"Did they talk about what was going on and who was involved in this?" O'Neal asked.

"He just told me that we was going to make some money."

"Did he tell about there's somebody in the store or something like that that was helping you or what?"

"This guy Robbie was supposed to set something up for them and everything."

The chain of command began to emerge: Archer set it up, Patrick pulled the trigger, Eddie drove the car, and Cliff was the other one inside Trout Auto with a ski mask. O'Neal asked Eddie when he first knew someone had been hurt or killed.

"After everything had happened, after it all happened, driving back, when they were complaining about blood and everything and talking about, you know," Eddie said, "Cliff said, 'He's gonna die' and all that kind of stuff and Pat shot him. And when Pat spent the night at my house, I asked Pat, I said, 'Pat, what exactly happened?' And he explained everything to me in detail."

Eddie recounted what Patrick said happened that night: "Pat walked up to the guy and the guy was complaining about he had kids and Pat said, 'I don't give a fuck.' He gave Cliff the gun and Cliff had his foot on the guy and was holding the gun to the guy's head and then Pat got all the money and he came back to Cliff and Cliff looked at Pat and said, 'Pat, he's gotta die,' and Pat goes, 'Give me the gun,' and he gave Pat the gun and Pat shot him in the head and then Pat said that's where all the blood came from and then that night was when I saw the blood after I got back to my house."

As Eddie described the events of that night, O'Neal was thinking, *No way he's telling the complete truth. This kid's not stupid. He says he didn't know anything about it, he's just the driver. But he brought a ski mask. You don't need a ski mask for a burglary. And he bought the bullets. Without the bullets, there's no murder.*

And there was something else—not so much what Eddie said as the way he said it. Nothing in Eddie's voice suggested that he knew he was in serious trouble. He seemed like a teenager telling a story about a night at the movies or taking a date to the mall.

Eddie was still thinking like a juvenile. O'Neal was thinking like an adult. Eddie's life was about action. O'Neal's was about consequences.

He doesn't get it, O'Neal thought. *Daddy's not going to get him out of this. He's not a juvenile anymore. He's going to Big Boy Jail.*

• • •

O'Neal was right. When he finished talking to the investigators at 6 P.M., Eddie was shocked that they didn't hand him over to his parents. Instead, they made him stand with his nose on the black dot painted on a column to have his profile photographed. He wouldn't be going home for dinner.

Charged with first-degree murder, Eddie was booked into the Escambia County Jail—a tall, gray, fortress-like building known to cops and inmates as Castle Grayskull. Eddie was fingerprinted, stripped of his clothes, and sprayed with disinfectant.

After he took off his clothes, Eddie folded them just as his mother taught him to do before putting them away in his bedroom dresser. The jailer gave him a paper sack for his belongings with his name written on the outside and his cell number: S41. Eddie tried to decipher the numbers. *Maybe*, he thought, *it means "Save for One Hour."*

He handed over his civilian clothes and received in return a pair of boxers, a pair of socks, a T-shirt, and a green jail jumpsuit three sizes too big. He handed the jumpsuit back, and they gave him one that more closely fit a skinny eighteen-year-old.

As O'Neal was questioning Eddie, Diana Fordham had been trying to find her son. She was making plans for dinner, and Eddie hadn't come home from work. She called the commissary, and they said Eddie had left with two plainclothes detectives. She called the sheriff's department, and they told her that he wasn't there and that they didn't know anything about his being arrested.

Shortly after 6 P.M., Tom Martin called Diana back and told her that Eddie was being charged with murder in the death of Billy Wayne Coker. Diana said that she and Larry were on their way to the sheriff's department. Martin told her that that would be unnecessary. Eddie had already given his statement and was being booked.

"Don't we have any say about the matter?" Diana said.

"No, you don't," Martin replied. "He's eighteen. He belongs to the state now."

Diana was still on the phone with Martin, crying, when her husband walked through the front door. When he asked Diana what was wrong, she handed him the phone. On the other end, Martin told Fordham that his son was being charged with Coker's murder.

"Well, he made his bed, he can sleep in it," Fordham said.

He immediately regretted his words.

. . .

From Eddie, O'Neal had what he needed to seek arrest warrants for Patrick Bonifay, Robin Archer, and Clifford Barth. Eddie confirmed what Jennifer Morris had said, that Patrick was the shooter, as well as what Wells suspected, that Archer set it up. And he knew the identity of the second man in the surveillance video: Clifford Barth.

O'Neal knew one other thing: he needed to move fast. The first suspect cannot be given time to warn the others. Eddie had already suggested that Patrick might run. O'Neal needed a judge to issue the arrest warrants. He found one in Circuit Judge Nicholas Geeker. While waiting for Geeker, O'Neal sent Cotton to find Patrick.

While Eddie was being booked into Castle Grayskull, Patrick was getting ready for night school. He'd asked Eddie to drive him from his mother's trailer in Brownsville to Escambia High, but when Eddie didn't show, Patrick's stepfather drove him. Following behind them was Cotton. On the way to the high school, O'Neal radioed Cotton that they had the arrest warrant for Patrick. Martin would meet him at the school.

From the parking lot, Cotton and Martin walked past the concrete green gator that guards the entrance to the school and the sign that proclaims Escambia High the "Home of Emmitt Smith," the University of Florida and Dallas Cowboys running back. They entered the terrazzo-and-brick front lobby the size of a dance floor, with glass cases crammed tight with trophies. To the right, down a hallway lined with the framed photos of Hall of Fame students, they found the night school principal.

. . .

Patrick was in his English class at 7:30 P.M. when the principal came to the door. After a few words were exchanged, the teacher pointed to Patrick and motioned to the principal. Patrick thought this was a good thing. He needed to talk to the principal about taking an American history class.

Martin and Cotton were waiting for Patrick outside the classroom.

The minute he stepped into the hallway, they told him he was under arrest for the murder of Billy Wayne Coker. They handcuffed him and led him out of the school and into Martin's car. On the way to the sheriff's department, Patrick denied knowing anything about Trout Auto and then fell silent.

"I don't know what you're talking about," he said to Martin.

In his silence, he told himself, *I'm done. My life is over.*

• • •

At the sheriff's department, Martin and Cotton maneuvered Patrick into the same office where Eddie had been questioned earlier. O'Neal was waiting for them. They put Patrick in the same chair that Eddie had sat in and handcuffed one wrist to the chair. O'Neal measured Patrick in his mind as if he were fitting him for a suit: *This kid's cocky. Thinks he's tough. We'll see how tough.*

"Look, we know what happened. We've already spoken to people," O'Neal told Patrick, and then laid it all out. Eddie had told them everything. Archer set it up, Eddie drove the car, Cliff went in the store, and Patrick killed Coker.

"You're getting the death penalty," O'Neal said. "You're going to death row for this. You're getting the chair."

Patrick shrugged.

"Alright," he said. "I'll talk."

O'Neal asked him if he wanted to call his mother.

"No," he replied. "I don't want her to know."

O'Neal found Patrick's remark as amazing as it was naive: *Geeze, by tomorrow everybody's going to know. This will be all over the news.*

With Patrick's refusal to call his mother, O'Neal had skirted the gray area of apprising juveniles of their right to notify their parents. State law requires police to notify the parents when they arrest a juvenile. But Martin and O'Neal knew what happens when you call the parents before questioning the child—they usually come running. In O'Neal's mind, the warrant for Patrick's arrest gave him the right to question Patrick without his parents' permission.

O'Neal gave Patrick his Miranda rights again and asked him to sign the waiver relinquishing those rights. Then he turned on the tape recorder at 9:07 P.M.

• • •

Patrick's mind was racing. He was thinking of what to say, who else they had talked to, how he could get out of this. Cutting through the panic in his head and the thumping of his heart, one thought surfaced like a drowning man's face breaking through the water: *They're going to kill me.*

Patrick believed that the only thing that would save him from the electric chair was to put it all on Archer, the only adult involved in the killing.

"Would you in just your own words, tell us again, what led up to the incident at Trout Auto Parts on W Street just about near midnight of January 26th, this year. What started the incident?" O'Neal asked.

"Okay," Patrick said. "My cousin, Robin Archer, he wanted me to do a hit on a person."

"Which person?"

"The person who worked at Trout Auto Parts."

"Okay, any particular night?"

"Friday night, midnight," Patrick said.

"The night before this incident?"

"Yes, sir."

"Did he tell you why?"

"Because the guy had got him fired and all, and just stuff like that."

"Okay. Did he tell you what he wanted you to do?"

"Yes, sir."

"What did he tell you to do?"

"Kill the man."

"Did he tell you any instructions or plans on how to, how you were supposed to do this?"

"I was supposed to walk up and get the man to go to the back and go through and wait on him to come through, and then one of us was supposed to do the man," Patrick said, but then added that Archer changed the plan. "He turned around and changed his mind and told us he just wanted us to walk up there and shoot him and kill him."

"Okay. Did he tell you where you were supposed to shoot him?"

"In the head."

"Okay. Who was with you when this happened?" O'Neal asked.

If it had been Kelly Bland or George Wynne, Patrick might have hesitated. He might have taken the fall himself, proved his loyalty, saved his friends. But it was Cliff and Eddie, and he knew already from O'Neal that they had talked to Eddie and Eddie gave him up.

"Eddie Fordham and Cliff Barth," he said.

After Patrick told O'Neal how he couldn't go through with it on Friday night, O'Neal asked him what changed his mind the following night. Patrick said Archer told him that if he loved his mom and girlfriend, he'd better do what he was supposed to do, or he'd be sorry.

"What was in it for you if you did it?" O'Neal asked.

"Supposedly a lot of money," Patrick replied. "Enough money to where I wouldn't have to worry about anything—anything else anymore."

They went back the next night, Patrick said—and then the words leaked out in spurts, punctuated with stifled sniffles as he struggled to hold the fluids, the tears and snot, inside his head. He spoke slowly in a low voice while inside his head a light flashed: *They're going to kill me. They're going to execute me.*

He could admit to what he did, but he couldn't admit he killed a man on his own. While he was outside the window, Patrick said, pointing the gun at Coker, Cliff came up and jarred him and the gun went off.

"He grabs me and the gun went off when I turned around and then, the man had fell. It had hit him and he started yelling . . . and Cliff started hollering, 'You didn't kill him . . . you didn't kill him.' So he took the gun and he leaned in and shot him again . . . and that didn't kill him neither . . . so we put our ski masks on and I went through the window first, you know, and I held the gun on him and you know he was sayin' . . . stuff like, you know, he had kids and all and I was just telling him to be quiet and you know . . . when he said, you know . . . please don't shoot me . . . and Cliff started hollerin', you know, 'I can't get the locks off.' So Cliff grabbed the gun . . . and I cut the locks off and then I climbed on top of the counter and cut the locks off, and I got the money and put it in a bag . . . and then, you know, when I got off the counter, Cliff goes, 'Patrick, kill him.' . . . so I take the gun from him and I stick it to his head . . . and I turn the other way and I pulled the trigger and Cliff started hollerin', 'Patrick he ain't dead' . . . so I shot him again . . . and then Cliff runs down the middle aisle because

he wasn't sure where to go and I said, 'This way, come on, hurry up.'
. . . so we go out the little door, and then we run out the door to go
outside, and I pull off my ski mask and Cliff pulled his off and we open
the door and I let the seat up and Cliff jumps in the back . . . and when
we get in the truck and all, I pull the gun out and I turned around and
I cocked it at Cliff, and I started yelling at him, Why, why did he, why
did he holler my name? Why did he have to do that? I didn't have to
kill the man. He had no reason to holler my name. We coulda just left
and everything would be okay."

. . .

O'Neal took notes as Patrick talked about how, the day after the murder, Archer showed up at the trailer, laughing, and telling Patrick he
wasn't going to get paid for killing the wrong guy.

By the time Patrick finished talking, twenty-three minutes later,
O'Neal's blank sheet of paper was filled with the basics of his case
against Patrick. Near the top, he wrote "When you shoot him, shoot
his head." Below that, "Box on wall—$30,000." And at the bottom,
underlined, "No $ killed wrong guy."

On paper, O'Neal had the facts. He had a clear mental picture of
Patrick: a savvy juvenile delinquent who knew the system, knew the
procedure, knew enough to shift the blame onto Cliff and the responsibility onto Archer. Kids like him, they don't think they'll get caught
and they don't think of what will happen when they do.

Patrick might have sniffled his way through his confession, but he
never broke down, never cried. Only after they handcuffed him again
and began to take him to booking on first-degree murder did he begin
to cry. He cried with the realization that he might never see Rachael
again.

. . .

After Patrick finished his confession, he took Cotton to the place off
Kingsfield Road where he and Eddie dumped the checks. Martin and
O'Neal went looking for Archer.

The only child of a maintenance man and a housewife, Archer had
started drinking at twelve and was expelled from school for chronic
truancy by the time he reached eighth grade. Since leaving home at

sixteen, Archer never had a place of his own. For a time he lived with Theresa and Howard Crenshaw and Patrick in the cramped trailer behind James Scarbrough's truck-refrigeration business. The night of the murder he was sleeping on a friend's couch.

Archer's '85 Nissan pickup matched the way he liked to dress: white pants, white shirt, like he was a man made of cocaine. In a sticker along the top of the windshield were the words "Snow White." The truck didn't have a door handle on the passenger side. Nobody got in or out unless Archer pushed a button on the dash that unlocked the door.

At 8:15 P.M., Martin and O'Neal found Archer's white Nissan parked outside his parents' house in Cantonment, a small community north of Pensacola. They arrested Archer for murder, handcuffed him, and slipped him into the backseat. Sullen and self-assured, he had little to say on the ride to the sheriff's department.

"You don't have anything on me. I've got an alibi," Archer said, adding that he was with his girlfriend that night.

The last thing he said was that he wanted to talk with his lawyer. They booked him directly into the jail.

• • •

Around 11 P.M., Martin and O'Neal arrived at the yellow-brick, three-bedroom rental house in Beulah on the outskirts of Pensacola where Clifford Barth was asleep in his bed.

Cliff's mother, Sheila, was watching TV when she heard the knock on the door. She opened it, and the two men in sport coats identified themselves as being with the Escambia County Sheriff's Department. They asked if they could come in.

"Is Cliff here?" O'Neal asked.

"Yes, he's in bed. He's asleep," Sheila replied.

"Can you wake him up?" O'Neal said.

"What for?"

"We want to see him."

Stunned, Sheila asked, "What has my son done?"

O'Neal asked her to take them to Cliff's bedroom.

When Cliff awoke, two men he didn't know were standing over him, his mother standing behind them. O'Neal told Cliff that they were arresting him for the Trout Auto Parts murder. In that moment, Sheila felt her heart stop and her mind go into hysterics. She started screaming.

Cliff got sick to his stomach. He had expected this day and feared this moment.

Just a week or so before, he had been at home alone eating a dinner of hot dogs and french fries and watching the local news when a story about the Trout Auto Parts murder came on the TV. On the screen flashed the sheriff's department's composite sketch of the suspicious kid that Wells said approached him at the parts window the night before the murder. The picture didn't look like Patrick, but it did look just like Cliff.

Cliff stopped chewing. A nausea rose from the pit of his stomach, like a punch to the gut. He spit the bite of hot dog onto the plate. The hunger he had felt a minute before vanished. He dumped his dinner in the garbage.

Now, at last, the police were here.

"I want to tell you the truth," Cliff told the officers. "I want to tell you what happened."

The deputies told him to get dressed, and Cliff asked his older sister, Angie, for a glass of water.

In the living room, as they handcuffed her son, Sheila was trying to figure out what to do. Her husband was at an Army base in Louisiana, her nineteen-year-old daughter had a baby, her brother Johnny— she'd call him. He would know what to do.

"Do I need to be down there?" she asked O'Neal.

It was just the kind of thing O'Neal liked to hear from a parent when he was arresting her child. Again, he had skirted the requirement of notifying the parents of their juvenile's arrest. Sheila knew her son was being arrested and passed on the opportunity to be there with him when they questioned him.

"No," O'Neal replied, "not at this point."

Cliff turned to his mother as they led him to the front door.

"Mom, don't worry."

During the drive to the sheriff's department, Cliff didn't say much. He stared out the window at the cars going by. He wondered if his mother was going to be okay and how his father would react. He didn't think about what he was going to tell the cops. On the night of the murder, when he got home, Cliff had stripped off his clothes and thrown them into a hamper. He jumped into the shower, but he couldn't wash away the feeling of being dirty. In the backseat of the sheriff's car, the dirty thing that lived inside him, the secret he dared not share, could finally be released. *It's over now*, he thought.

At the station, after Cliff was handcuffed to a chair, they told him the story they'd heard earlier from Patrick, that Cliff had shot the clerk during the robbery. They made it clear: Coker was dead, and Cliff was facing the death penalty in his murder.

In his mind, Cliff couldn't believe what he was hearing. *I didn't kill anybody*.

Cliff answered all the questions with a sad resolve. His remorse impressed O'Neal. Here, finally, was a kid who knew that what he had done was wrong and felt genuinely bad about it.

Cliff's recorded statement took seven minutes.

He told them of driving to Trout Auto Parts on Saturday, January 26, close to midnight. The words spilled out of him like water through a broken pipe.

The last thing he said before they turned off the tape recorder was: "I didn't pull the trigger."

• • •

By the time O'Neal pulled into his driveway, it was after 1 A.M. There was still much to do. He needed to find the gun, interview George Wynne, and talk with Kelly Bland again. But that was for another day. He was exhausted and exhilarated. Tonight, he had solved his first murder case.

• • •

Despite its reverence for the past, Pensacola also envisioned itself a modern American city. One block west of where the city originated—almost in defiance of the ornate architecture surrounding Plaza Ferdinand VII—Escambia County erected the unadorned M. C. Blanchard Judicial Building. It was built like a bunker, all flat concrete walls, straight lines, and sharp edges. The architects gave the building one distinguishing feature—a staggered top floor that jutted out like drawers pulled out of a bedroom dresser. When the courthouse opened in 1978, it was acclaimed for being distinctive, contemporary, and modern.

To those who worked inside, the courthouse was a no-nonsense building in a city where justice came quickly. Murder trials in Pensacola took days, not weeks. Sleek, modern, and efficient fit Special Prosecutor P. Michael Patterson just fine. The Pensacola-born Patterson, who went to law school in Gainesville and came back home to practice, was good at seeing things in straight lines and sharp divisions. Good and bad. Just and unjust. Guilty and not guilty. Ambiguity was his enemy in the courtroom. Doubt, even the shadow of it, was intolerable.

As soon as O'Neal handed him the evidence in the Trout Auto Parts murder case, Patterson felt he could convict all four defendants. His greatest challenge would be persuading a jury to sentence a seventeen-year-old boy to death. Of the 171 men awaiting the electric chair on Florida's death row in 1991, only one was seventeen at the time of his conviction. Patterson was determined to make Patrick Bonifay the second.

Eddie Fordham's house.

Clifford Barth's house.

Patrick Bonifay's grandfather's house.

Trout Auto Parts building.

Billy Wayne Coker wearing policeman's uniform. Photo obtained from attorney Martin Levin.

Billy Wayne Coker's trailer.

Exterior of Trout Auto Parts and chute window. Photo from Escambia County Circuit Criminal Court.

Interior of chute window. Photo from Escambia County Circuit Criminal Court.

Gun provided to Patrick Bonifay by Kelly Bland. Photo from Escambia County Circuit Criminal Court.

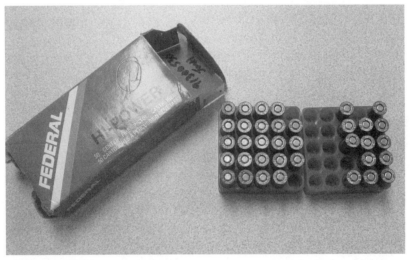

Bullets purchased by Eddie Fordham and Patrick Bonifay. Photo from Escambia County Circuit Criminal Court.

Blue book bag and bolt cutters supplied by Bonifay. Photo from Escambia County Circuit Criminal Court.

Sketch of suspect based on Daniel Wells's description. Image from Escambia County Circuit Criminal Court.

Escambia County Jail (Castle Grayskull).

M. C. Blanchard Judicial Building.

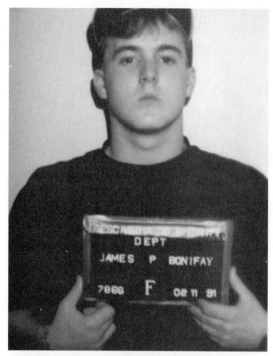

Patrick Bonifay. Photo
from Escambia County
Sheriff's Office.

Eddie Fordham. Photo
from Escambia County
Sheriff's Office.

Clifford Barth. Photo from Escambia County Sheriff's Office.

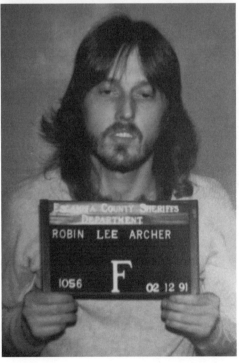

Robin Lee Archer. Photo from Escambia County Sheriff's Office.

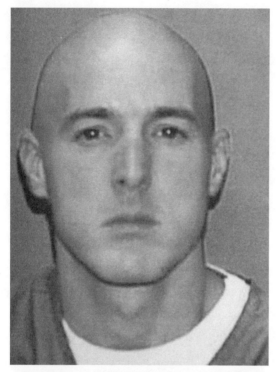

Patrick Bonifay, 2011.
Photo from Florida Department of Corrections.

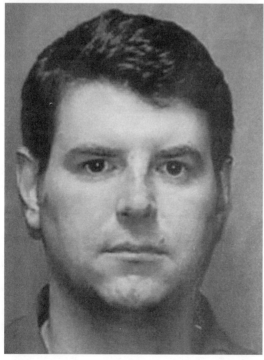

Eddie Fordham, 2011.
Photo from Florida Department of Corrections.

Clifford Barth, 2011.
Photo from Florida
Department of Correc-
tions.

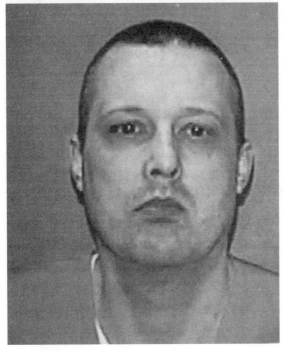

Robin Lee Archer, 2011.
Photo from Florida
Department of Correc-
tions.

Act Negates Age 5

On the evening of March 6, 1978, two teenagers walked through the subway cars of the A train in Manhattan looking for sleeping passengers to rob. One, fifteen-year-old Willie Bosket, carried in his back pocket a medium-length Double O Seven switchblade on a horsehide string. His older cousin, Herman Spates, was with him as they walked past dozing passengers, casually kicking their feet to see if they were awake.

Spates, abandoned by his parents before the age of sixteen, had grown up on the streets of New York, sleeping in movie theaters, making his living robbing people and burglarizing buildings. He had been arrested six times since he turned sixteen.

Willie was a small, cherub-faced boy who grew up in the juvenile detention facilities of New York State. His father, Butch Bosket, was in prison for murdering a Milwaukee pawnbroker and a customer. Rejected by his mother, Willie seemed determined, at an early age, to emulate his father.

Willie had recently been released from reform school, where he had terrorized the staff with his fits of destructive violence. Every adult who tried to help him was confounded by the contrast between his outwardly angelic appearance and his inner rage. To Willie, violence wasn't just an act of survival; it was the essence of life itself. In his world, violence was a code of conduct, and he carried that mentality to the extreme.

As the A train pulled into the 207th Street station, the last stop on the line, Willie nudged the foot of a woman slumped in her seat. When she didn't open her eyes, he went through her pockets, finding them empty.

Leaving the train, the two boys were arrested by a pair of Transit Authority officers for attempted robbery. Willie was taken to the underground Transit office, where he was handcuffed to a bench in the locker room. The police called his mother.

When she arrived, Laura Bosket was furious.

"Get your ass over here right now," she said.

Willie, his face in a pout, ignored her.

"Didn't I say get your ass over here?" his mother said. "And straighten out that face. You always getting in trouble. One of these days, I ain't going to come, and your ass is going to end up dead or right in jail."

Released to his mother, Willie was soon back on the subways. This time he was alone, and this time he had a gun. He had bought the gun from his mother's boyfriend for sixty-five dollars, paid for with money he had stolen from the wallet of a sleeping passenger. Willie bought a holster for the brown-handled, steel-blue .22 so he could strap it to his hip like the cop he fantasized becoming. When he wore the gun, his walk became a strut.

It was 5:30 P.M. on March 19 when Willie stepped onto the Number 3 IRT train. He spotted a sleeping Hispanic man wearing pink sunglasses and a gold digital watch. Willie was alone in the car with the middle-aged man. He kicked the man's feet. No response. Willie drew his gun. But as he tried to slip the watch off the man's wrist, the man suddenly woke up. Willie didn't hesitate. He shot the man through the sunglasses in the right eye. The man threw his hands up and screamed. Blood was spurting from his face.

If he's not dead, he's going to cause me a problem, Willie thought.

Willie aimed the gun at the man's head and pulled the trigger. The man fell back and slumped to the floor of the subway car. Willie took the watch from the man's wrist, a ring from his finger, and fifteen dollars from his wallet. He stepped off the subway at the Lenox Avenue terminal and walked coolly down the street, where he sold the ring for twenty dollars.

At home, he showed his sister the watch, which had blood on it.

"Booby," she said, "where'd you get that watch?"

"I killed a motherfucker," he said, laughing.

Willie Bosket, who had been in juvenile facilities since he was nine years old, had often wondered what it felt like to kill someone. Now he knew. It felt like no big deal.

The newspapers identified the man he killed as Noel Perez, the apparent victim of a random shooting.

A week later, March 27, Willie and Herman jumped the turnstile at the 135th Street station and boarded the Number 3 train. There was only one other passenger in the car, a Hispanic man in his mid-thirties. Willie posted Herman by the front of the car and approached the man. He put the barrel of the gun three inches from the man's head.

"Give up your money," he ordered.

"I ain't got any," the man replied.

Willie pulled the trigger. The man slipped off the seat and onto the floor, faceup in a pool of his blood. Herman bolted. Willie calmly bent down and went through the man's pockets. He found a wallet with a city welfare card and two one-dollar bills. The welfare card identified the man as Moises Perez.

When Willie met up with Herman, they tossed the wallet behind a bowling alley and walked back to Willie's house. Willie was giggling. He felt no remorse. Whatever empathy he might once have had for other people had been leached from his conscience by a childhood spent in state institutions and on the streets of New York, where being the best meant being the most merciless.

Willie Bosket, at age fifteen, had become what he had long aspired to be: a big-time killer.

His arrest four days later made the front-page news, giving Willie the fame he so desired. The public was shocked that a boy so young could have committed such brutal murders. Shock turned to outrage when, under state law, Willie was sentenced to five years for the two murders—the maximum he could receive under New York's juvenile justice system. Willie would be free when he reached twenty-one in December 1983.

In response, Governor Hugh Carey pressed the state legislature to pass the country's first law that allowed juveniles to be tried as adults for violent crimes. Under the Juvenile Offender Act of 1978, juveniles as young as thirteen could be tried in criminal court for murder and face the same punishment as adults. The New York law marked a break from the Progressive tradition, which since the turn of the century had maintained that children were different from adults and capable of rehabilitation. Bad kids, the new thinking said, were no different from bad adults. They needed to be locked up and punished, not reformed.

Willie became the nation's poster child for the notion that there was a new breed of kid without fear or conscience preying on the public. New York's "Willie Bosket law" became the model for other states, including Florida.

Three years later, the Sunshine State joined the wave of states passing laws making it easier to try juveniles as adults, giving prosecutors the ability to bypass judges and "direct file" teenagers sixteen and older.

Public alarm over violent acts by teenagers convinced lawmakers that the juvenile justice system created by Progressives such as Chicago's Jane Addams, Lucy Flower, and Julia Lathrop was ill-equipped to handle a new breed of juvenile criminal—the "super-predator" who, despite his age, needed to be locked up forever. These weren't kids stealing hubcaps and getting into fistfights. They were youths who settled arguments with guns. The system designed for the Bowery Boys didn't work for Crips and Bloods. These kids had no respect for authority—cops, teachers, or parents—and were sophisticated in their manipulation of a juvenile system that was built for reforming rather than punishing. They were old enough to know right from wrong, and callous enough not to care. "Adult time for adult crimes" became the mantra for law enforcement and legislators who advocated "zero tolerance" for youthful offenders. In the last decade of the twentieth century, the United States had returned, full circle, to the

1800s, when children committing crimes were considered the same as adults.

With the new legislation, the distinction between adult and adolescent blurred. With every attempt to establish a bright line of demarcation separating juveniles from grown-ups, there was the acknowledgment that the number was arbitrary. One day a person was a juvenile, the next day an adult. Other than a birthday cake, nothing had changed—and yet everything had changed.

In Florida, the crisis of confidence in the juvenile justice system coincided with a loss of confidence in the parole system. At the same time the state was making it easier to charge juveniles as adults, it was also abolishing parole for Florida inmates. In 1983 the state legislature, responding to public pressure over inconsistent and lenient sentencing by judges and the release of violent prisoners, replaced parole with mandatory sentences. A juvenile or adult convicted of a serious crime would be sentenced to serious time of a fixed duration with no opportunity for early release through parole. There was one exception: murder.

In the summer of 1991, as Patrick, Eddie, and Cliff awaited trial, the penalty for murder was execution or life with the possibility of parole after twenty-five years. For Patrick and Cliff, the determination of whether they would be indicted as adults for Coker's murder was in the hands of a grand jury convened by Special Prosecutor Michael Patterson.

It would not be a difficult decision.

The Trial 6

Pensacolans were appalled by the brutality of Coker's murder, and alarmed that high school kids had been arrested for his death. Pensacola's Channel 3 ran a special called "Why Children Kill." The people of Pensacola wanted revenge. It was Michael Patterson's job to give it to them.

Patterson embraced the power of his position. He liked being at the controls of criminal justice. He believed that the prosecutor's duty was more than putting criminals in prison. The prosecutor was the gatekeeper, the one who stands at the door and decides who goes to trial and who doesn't, who goes to jail and who gets to go free, who serves life in prison and who dies in the electric chair. He was the arbiter of right and wrong. The responsibility fit him like a tailored suit.

Moments like this were why Patterson loved being a prosecutor. After graduating from the University of Florida Law School in 1973, he had spent nine years in private practice, and briefly as a defense attorney. The other side liked what they saw and recruited him to join the state attorney's office. He decided to take the job after his little boy asked him what he did for a living. The best answer, Patterson decided when he agreed to become a prosecutor, was that he was the guardian of justice.

In another case, under different circumstances, Patterson might have decided that one mad, impulsive moment in a teenager's day should not determine his life forever. Patterson knew something about teenagers—their impulsiveness, their immaturity, their inability to see beyond the moment. He had his own teenage son at home about the same age as Patrick and Cliff.

But this wasn't one of those times. The case against Patrick, handed to him by O'Neal, was a premeditated mistaken-identity murder for money inflicted upon an unintended victim who was shot to death while begging for his life.

Charging youths as adults was commonplace in Florida; sending teens to death row was not. Florida had no age limit on the death penalty, but sentencing teenagers to death was becoming increasingly rare. The only person on death row who had been a teenager at the time of his conviction was Cleo LeCroy, who was seventeen when he was arrested for killing a young Palm Beach couple on a camping trip on January 4, 1981.

The last time Florida executed a teenager was in 1944, the same year South Carolina electrocuted fourteen-year-old George Stinney— the youngest person executed in the twentieth century.

Patrick was forty-seven days beyond his seventeenth birthday when he killed Coker. To Patterson, the act alone turned Patrick from a boy into a man.

Patterson had tried more difficult cases before, but to convince a jury that Patrick's age was irrelevant he needed the testimony of the other teenagers who were with him that night—he needed Patrick's friends. He went to Eddie Fordham first.

• • •

Of the three teenagers' families, only Eddie's could afford to hire a lawyer. Larry Fordham Sr. was an ambitious, successful insurance man who owned his own business with Globe Life. Diana worked as hard to advance her husband's career as Larry did to make money. She volunteered in political campaigns and entertained. The Fordhams belonged to the social circle in Pensacola that staged a Mardi Gras parade and ball every year. The night of the Trout Auto murder, Diana was performing a skit she had written for the grand ball.

But the Fordhams had trouble finding a lawyer to take Eddie's case. Larry approached several lawyers in town. It would cost him $30,000 to $50,000, they told him. And then they gave him some free legal advice: Save your money for an appeals attorney. These boys are going to be convicted. Everyone knew the case. Everyone knew the judge: Lacey Collier, a get-tough-on-crime judge.

Collier was typical of a breed of transplanted Pensacola residents who trained at the Naval Air Station and came back after leaving the military. So many airmen, Navy guys, and admirals married Pensacola women that the city started calling itself the "Mother-in-law of the U.S. Navy." Born in Demopolis, Alabama, Collier trained as a pilot in Pensacola and returned to get his bachelor's degree from the city's University of West Florida in 1975. After getting a law degree from Florida State, he returned again to work as a state attorney until becoming a circuit judge in 1984.

Collier was a tough-minded judge who ran a tight courtroom. Although he had a reputation as being a fair and efficient judge, some defense attorneys complained that he was impatient, inflexible, and stubborn. He made up his mind quickly and then stuck to it. And one more thing: Collier was up for appointment to the federal courts. This could be the case that made him a federal judge.

Pensacola's legal circle was small and intimate. Just about everyone who practiced criminal law knew the kind of lawyer Patterson was and the strength of his case against Eddie, Patrick, Cliff, and Archer. Under Florida's felony murder law, anyone involved in a killing is as guilty of murder as the one who pulls the trigger. In their statements to police, Patrick, Eddie, and Cliff all admitted to being at Trout Auto the night Coker was killed. Under felony murder, it didn't matter whether they knew someone was going to be killed. Even experienced defense attorneys knew how hard it would be to win this case.

Eddie ended up with Assistant Public Defender Elton Killam, who knew Eddie's father—he and Larry had attended Escambia High School together. Killam felt he was doing a former classmate a favor by representing Eddie, even though he remembered Larry as something of a bully in high school—pushy, aggressive, egotistical.

Killam also knew Patterson from their days growing up in Pensacola and from the short time they had spent together in the public defender's office in the 1970s. Killam knew both the case and Patterson well enough to believe that Eddie's best chance was to turn state's witness and testify against Patrick. As Killam saw it, Eddie was the driver, and it wasn't unusual for the wheelman in a murder to testify in exchange for a lesser sentence. Killam knew how Patterson liked it—to meet face-to-face with a client. Alone. This had worked for Killam in the past with the adults he had represented. He had no reason to believe it wouldn't work with a teenager like Eddie. So Killam set up a meeting for Eddie and Patterson at the Escambia County Jail.

• • •

About three months after his arrest, Eddie was escorted by his lawyer into a small interview room inside the county jail. The room was just big enough for a rectangular table, a few chairs, and a phone on the wall. The walls were stark. The door was solid metal with a small window carved into the middle.

The minute Patterson walked in, Eddie felt intimidated. Patterson was a tall, confident forty-two-year-old man; Eddie was a skinny, scared eighteen-year-old boy. After introducing his client to the prosecutor, Killam glanced at his watch and excused himself. Eddie felt like a sheep in the same cage as a wolf, shoved in there by his own lawyer.

Eddie pushed aside the uneasy feeling of being left alone with Patterson and the sense of abandonment by Killam for the chance to tell the prosecutor exactly what happened that night. "The truth will set you free," Eddie's father had told him. Eddie thought that that was what Patterson wanted to hear: The truth, the whole truth, not the messy, mixed-up truth that spilled all over the table the night Tom O'Neal took his statement.

Eddie told Patterson he'd been duped by Patrick, who intentionally didn't tell him what was going on that night. He thought Patrick was going into Trout Auto to complete a drug deal set up by Archer. He didn't know there was going to be a robbery, didn't know anyone was going to be killed, didn't know Patrick had a gun.

Patterson looked annoyed. The more Eddie tried to explain, the more impatient Patterson became. Eddie began to feel frustrated himself. The whole time Eddie was talking, Patterson was pacing back and forth in the space between the table and the wall. He stopped, put his hands on the table, and leaned toward Eddie. Patterson wanted information Eddie didn't have that would help connect Patrick to Archer and Archer's plan to kill the clerk at Trout Auto. Did Eddie see Patrick give any of the money to Archer? Did Eddie hear Patrick and Archer talking about the plan to kill the clerk? He wanted Eddie to help him put a noose around Patrick's neck, but he offered little in return— no promise that, if Eddie testified, Patterson would drop the charges against him, no assurances that he would receive a reduced sentence in exchange for his cooperation. The one thing Patterson offered Eddie was the chance to avoid the death penalty.

If Eddie said he didn't know something, Patterson asked him to think harder. Eddie felt Patterson didn't want the truth at all. Eddie wasn't going to lie. He wasn't a robber. He wasn't a killer. He was just the driver—Patrick's wheelman.

"I'm sorry, but I cannot testify and tell you what you want to hear," Eddie said. "If I get on the stand I'm going to tell it like it is."

Patterson didn't get what he hoped for from Eddie that day, but he didn't slam the door on the way out. He left it open with the suggestion that Eddie, when he got back to his cell, should think long and hard about what he knew that might help convict Patrick.

• • •

Patterson had gone into the meeting thinking Eddie was willing to cooperate. He knew something about Eddie. This wasn't the first time the boy had been in trouble. There was the joyriding in his father's boat and the stolen Jet Ski, and, before that, the time Eddie was arrested after he broke into an auto-salvage business with one of the Brown Boyz and made off with $17,000 in high-performance auto parts. That time, when the cops came and got him out of class, Eddie's father was waiting outside.

Patterson had read the statement Eddie gave O'Neal the night of his arrest, in which Eddie said that he knew there was going to be a robbery at Trout Auto, that he supplied a ski mask and bought the bullets, that he saw the bolt cutters, that he knew someone had been killed, and that he took the money and spent some of it the next day with Patrick at the mall.

But inside the small interview room at the county jail, Eddie told Patterson a different story. He brought the mask because Patrick told him he wanted to scare their girlfriends. He bought the bullets because Patrick said he wanted to do some target practice at Cliff's place. The bolt cutters were for a burglary of an old man's house that Patrick had planned that night. Trout Auto was a drug deal.

Patterson didn't believe a word of it. *He thinks he's in control*, Patterson thought. *I can tell you what I want to tell you. I'm really good at talking, and I can just talk my way out of this.*

Eddie didn't appear scared or intimidated to Patterson. He seemed smug, almost arrogant, and naive enough to think he could spin a tale of ignorance and innocence and make the prosecutor believe it.

Patterson told Eddie he didn't need his testimony. He had all the evidence he needed to convict all four of them. He was giving him a chance, doing him a favor. "It's in your best interest to tell the truth," Patterson said. "You need to tell me everything you know. You need to give me everything you remember about what happened."

Eddie stuck to his story that he knew nothing of the plan to rob Trout Auto and kill the clerk.

Eddie was under the mistaken impression that there was a negotiation going on here, Patterson concluded. Patterson, the prosecutor, doesn't bargain. He doesn't offer reduced charges or lesser sentences in exchange for testimony. In his experience, state's witnesses can do as much harm as good. He saw jurors take a dislike to the state's witness. He lost cases that way. Eddie might be that kind of witness, more trouble than help.

Eddie didn't get it, Patterson decided. He was the pampered and protected little rich kid who had been in trouble before and always had Daddy there to bail him out. In Patterson's opinion, Eddie wasn't willing to admit what he did, take responsibility for his actions, and accept the consequences.

After getting nowhere with Eddie, Patterson tried to talk to Eddie's father. Maybe the father could talk some sense into the son. Their encounter was disastrous. If Eddie seemed smug, his father appeared defiant. Larry professed complete and absolute faith in his son. If Eddie said he didn't know a thing, then that was true. He could not tell his child to testify to anything but the truth. He would not advise his son to tell a lie to save his own skin.

Fine. Patterson didn't need Eddie. He still had Cliff.

. . .

Later that month, Cliff and Patrick were in the juvenile section of the county jail when Cliff's court-appointed lawyer, Michael Allen, showed up with Patterson. Seeing his lawyer and the prosecutor together made Cliff nervous. Allen hadn't said anything to Cliff about meeting with Patterson. After the two men led Cliff to a small interview room, Allen introduced Cliff to Patterson and then excused himself, saying he had other appointments. Before he left he offered his client some legal advice: Go ahead and answer whatever questions Mr. Patterson has.

Cliff felt confused and uneasy in the presence of the prosecutor. Patterson was tall, dark-haired, and impeccably dressed in a dark suit. To Cliff, seated at a table in the small room, Patterson appeared imposing. Cliff had never met Patterson before, but he knew him by reputation. Cliff braced himself for an aggressive interrogation.

Instead, Patterson came across as friendly, sympathetic, and understanding. The prosecutor had a down-home quality that made Cliff feel he was easy to talk to.

Patterson laid it all out for him: You were inside Trout Auto, you held the gun on Coker, Patrick said you shot Coker, and you were there when he was murdered. You're facing the death penalty. And then Patterson explained why he was there to talk with Cliff: He wanted Cliff's cooperation in testifying against Patrick, Eddie, and Archer. In return for Cliff's cooperation, Patterson would not seek the death penalty. If he chose not to cooperate, it was Patterson's job to prove his guilt and, with his conviction, send him to the electric chair. He told Cliff one other thing, the same thing he had told Eddie: I really don't need you. I have enough evidence to convict you, Patrick, and everyone else, whether you agree to cooperate or not.

Filled with thoughts of his own death, Cliff could think of no alternative but to do whatever Patterson asked. *I'm seventeen years old. I don't want to die*, he thought. Patterson offered one more assurance in exchange for his cooperation: Regardless of what Cliff testified to in the trials of Patrick, Eddie, and Archer, he would not use his words against him in his own trial. This seemed significant to Cliff, who was convinced that he would be acquitted in front of his own jury.

In that first meeting, Cliff did exactly what his attorney advised: He answered every question Patterson asked. They went over the details of the murder, all the evidence that Patterson had collected and needed Cliff to corroborate. They would meet several more times. Sometimes Patterson brought his secretary along to take notes. Cliff's attorney was never present. In preparing for the trials of Patrick, Eddie, and Archer, Cliff spent many more hours with Patterson than he would with his own attorney in preparing his own defense.

. . .

Patterson liked Cliff the moment he met him. Cliff was remorseful and painfully, genuinely guilt-stricken for what he had done to Coker's family and his own parents. Patterson found him to be candid, honest, and straightforward. There didn't seem to be any calculation behind his recounting of the events that night and his own responsibility in Coker's death. In Patterson's mind, Cliff was as credible as Eddie was unbelievable.

To Patterson, they were all just kids—Cliff, Eddie, and Patrick—but only Cliff seemed to recognize what he had done and appreciate its seriousness. Patterson felt that, if not for that one night, that momentary lapse of juvenile judgment, Cliff's life might have taken an entirely different direction. Of the three, Cliff acted the most like an adult.

. . .

The sky was partly cloudy, the temperature starting its steady climb to ninety-five degrees on the morning of July 15, 1991, as Patterson rode the elevator from his first-floor state attorney's office to Courtroom 401 on the fourth floor of the M. C. Blanchard Judicial Building. He wore a plain white shirt (as he always did for court), tasseled loafers, and a dark suit that his wife might have helped him pick out at a shopping mall department store like Dillard's or Macy's.

Courtroom 401 was a windowless jewel box of light-wood paneling and burgundy-upholstered spectators' chairs arranged in a semicircle, lit by bright fluorescent lights. The courtroom occupied a corner of the top floor of the squat, four-story complex of courtrooms and judicial offices in the Blanchard Building.

Patterson felt at home here. As special prosecutor he had tried more than a hundred cases, fifteen or so of them murders, in the Blanchard courthouse. He could count on one hand the number of trials he lost and the number of times he had a conviction overturned and still have fingers left over. That's how it should be, Patterson felt. A good prosecutor should win because those on trial are guilty; if they're innocent, they shouldn't be prosecuted in the first place.

High-profile, time-consuming cases were Patterson's forte. He had tried the case of another teenager who got his fifteen-year-old girlfriend pregnant and then hacked her to pieces with a machete on Pensacola Beach. He found the murder weapon by enlisting a local metal-detector club to search the dunes. He prosecuted the killers of Mildred Baker, Derek Hill, Michael Douglass, and Michael McCormack in 1989, sending Timothy Robinson and Michael Coleman to death row and Darrell Frazier to prison for life.

The key to success in the courtroom, Patterson believed, was to be better prepared than the opposing counsel. A conviction was 99 percent preparation and 1 percent courtroom performance. He often got involved in the investigation soon after the crime was committed. He might show up while the crime scene was still hot. He made sure the evidence was processed correctly and handled properly. He sometimes interviewed witnesses himself.

And now he was standing before the judge and jury, prepared to try a kid for killing a clerk. Patterson felt confident in his preparation, but he was a little nervous, like the straight-A student about to take an exam. With a jury there was always some uncertainty about the outcome, no matter how good a case or how strong the evidence.

The small knot inside his stomach didn't show on the face he presented to the jury. Patterson had learned over the years to exude confidence and authority. He never stood behind the podium with sheaves of papers or a big yellow legal pad. He always used three-by-five note cards containing a few words that served as prompts to his preparation. The note cards showed the jury, and the opposition, that Michael Patterson was in command.

Dressed in a purple sweatshirt, Patrick was seated next to his court-appointed attorney, Ted Stokes, at a table on the left side of the court-room. Patrick's mother, Theresa, sat a few rows behind him. Patterson and his assistants sat at the table to the right. Sandra Coker found a seat behind them and across the aisle from Theresa.

Judge Collier presided from a leather chair flanked by the flags of Florida and the United States. The jury of three men and eleven women, two of them alternates, sat in the box to the left, near the defense table.

The trial lasted two days. Patterson called sixteen witnesses. Stokes called none.

Cliff was Patterson's tenth witness. To convince the jury that Patrick was guilty and deserving of the death penalty, Patterson needed to prove that there was intent to kill, that it was done for money, and that the killing was merciless. Cliff's testimony provided him with evidence of all three.

● ● ●

On the stand, Cliff avoided looking at Patrick, who was seated at the defense table. He didn't glance at the jury or look at the curved rows of spectators. He was afraid that if he looked around he'd freeze up, get confused, and screw up an answer. He felt his stomach flutter, his heart race, dampness forming on the palms of his hands. He had never liked being the focus of attention, and this was like being on a stage illuminated by a spotlight. All he could think of was getting this over with as quickly as possible.

Patterson asked him what happened after the murder when Cliff was dividing up the money with Patrick and Eddie.

"Was Mr. Bonifay real upset?" Patterson said.

"Not really."

"Well, was he laughing or crying or what?" Patterson pressed.

He was excited, Cliff replied. They all were. The adrenaline was flowing.

"Mr. Bonifay was laughing?" Patterson asked.

"He wasn't really laughing," Cliff said, "but just snickering."

"Snickering?"

"Uh-huh."

When it was Stokes's turn, he asked Cliff if Patrick appeared to be stoned the night of the murder. Patrick had told his attorney that he was high on a joint laced with cocaine.

"Not really," Cliff replied.

"Did he have some problems once he got inside Trout Auto Parts when he was trying to climb up on that counter? Did he have some problems stumbling around?"

"Yeah, he almost fell."

"Did that make you think he might be stoned?"

"No, I didn't really think about it."

On re-examination, Patterson asked Cliff whether Patrick had ever talked to him about saying he was stoned the night of the murder. Cliff said yes. Patterson asked him when that conversation took place.

"This morning," Cliff replied.

"Did he appear high to you?" Patterson asked.

"He acted normal to me."

• • •

As he sat next to his attorney, Patrick listened to Cliff's testimony with one thought in his mind: *This dude is trying to get me killed.* Cliff's testimony felt like a fist to the stomach and a slap to the face, orchestrated by Patterson to convince the jury that Patrick was a monster who deserved to die. It was Cliff talking, but he was only saying what Patterson wanted him to say. Patrick felt no sense of betrayal by Cliff, because there was no loyalty to begin with. The betrayal came from Kelly Bland, who had testified earlier. His best friend had provided him with the gun and then turned state's witness to save his own skin. What hurt most was when Kelly, whose life he had saved twice, denied on the stand that they had ever been friends.

But when Cliff testified that Patrick had told him the same morning to lie about Patrick's being high, it angered him enough to lean over to Stokes and tell his lawyer that that was a brazen lie, and they could prove it. How could Cliff say they had spoken that morning when they were kept in separate parts of the jail, precisely so that they couldn't talk?

Patrick told Stokes to ask the judge for a recess and call over to the jail to get the records that would show he couldn't possibly have told Cliff anything that morning. Stokes brushed the suggestion aside. "Oh, don't worry about it," he said. That seemed to be his stock answer whenever Patrick tried to participate in his own defense: Don't worry about it.

Patrick knew then that it was over.

In his closing statements to the jury the next day, Stokes used a strategy that even Patrick, hearing it for the first time, found bizarre. By this time, Patrick had lost all confidence in and respect for his attorney. To him, his court-appointed lawyer looked fat, slovenly, and inept. His breath smelled bad. Stokes had spent little time with him discussing defense strategy, and even less preparing Patrick for what he was about to tell the jury before their deliberations.

The trial of James Patrick Bonifay, Stokes told the jurors, reminded him of the war in Iraq against Saddam Hussein.

"We have in this case a young man, Patrick Bonifay, and you also saw Mr. Barth, who testified in the case, and there was another young man, Eddie Fordham, who were really the foot soldiers of a war," Stokes said. "We have people like Robin Archer who were sitting back as kingpin and King Saddam Hussein, if you will, and sending these young boys, these kids out to do their work, just as Saddam Hussein sent out teenage boys as the foot soldiers out to do his work."

Stokes knew that, more than the trial of three kids accused of a murder, what was on most people's minds in the summer of 1991 was the Gulf War. Trout Auto had been a front-page story for a few days six months ago, but Desert Storm was in the news every day. Pensacola was a military town of sailors and pilots, many of them deployed to Kuwait and Iraq, and Pensacolans followed the details of the war like some folks watch the Weather Channel.

As he presented his closing argument, Stokes switched from war to chess. The teenage soldiers became pawns.

"Eddie Fordham and Clifford Barth and Patrick Bonifay are nothing more than pawns in a chess game. I don't know if any of you people play chess or if you ever have. I haven't played it in a long time, but

I remember that you put the pawns out front," Stokes argued. "You know pawns can only move one way. They can only move forward. Patrick Bonifay tried to reverse that and he tried to come back. He came back and the king, who was Robin Archer, said no, you can't come back. You're a pawn. You have to go forward."

When it was his turn, Patterson stepped before the jury with the purpose of returning them to reality.

"At the onset let me remind you, and I think the judge will remind you, that your verdict should be based on the evidence, not on fantasy, not on the Persian Gulf War, but on the evidence that's been received in this case," Patterson said. "The threat against Mr. Bonifay, let me respond to that just briefly. That is a story that this man made up, one of many stories that this man made up in an effort to avoid responsibility for what he knew he did. And he cooked up several of them. You heard some of them. He will use whatever means necessary. He will whimper and cry if he thinks it will help him. He will do anything to avoid responsibility for what he knows he did."

Stokes talked about playing chess. Patterson did play chess. He had played a lot of it as a teenager, and although he never got really good at the game, it did teach him how to think ahead. As a seasoned prosecutor, he knew how to anticipate the next move of the defense and how a jury might react to a piece of evidence. He couldn't be certain, but he felt confident that the jury would convict Patrick, so as he presented them with the evidence of Patrick's guilt he also laid the foundation for his argument for the death penalty—while pretending not to.

"You should not convict the defendant at this stage of the trial because in his explanation to the police—in the opportunity he had to say anything about this he wanted to say—his only expression of concern about what happened was that he was afraid he was going to lose his girlfriend. That was his expression of concern. Not for Mr. Coker or for what he had done or for his family. His expression of concern is what's happening to me, gosh, I might lose my girlfriend over this. You should not convict him for that reason," Patterson said.

"You should not convict him because he is snickering in the car after he has killed Mr. Coker and dividing the money and laughing about it. You should not convict him at this stage of the trial for that.

"You should not convict him because he cussed at Mr. Coker when Mr. Coker was begging for his life and saying I have a wife and children and he scoffed and cursed his wife and children. You should not convict him at this stage of the trial for that.

"You should not convict him because he killed Mr. Coker while he was begging for his life. This is not the stage of the trial that you should use those things against the defendant. I believe you will have an opportunity to consider those facts in making another decision."

The next day, July 17, the jury began its deliberations. Within an hour, they came back. Their decision remained sealed pending the trial of Robin Lee Archer, which began the same day.

• • •

Without knowing his own fate, Patrick took the stand against Archer, who, dressed in a blue shirt and white tie, occupied the same seat at the same table where Patrick had sat earlier that day.

The evidence Patterson presented Archer's jury with was tenuous. He showed that Archer gave Patrick the gun that killed Coker, but the gun came from Bland, not Archer. He provided friends and associates of Archer who testified that Robbie told them he knew what was going to happen at Trout Auto and who did it, but none of them directly implicated Archer as the one who hired Patrick to commit a murder.

The only one who could directly tie Archer to Coker's death was the same person Patterson was determined to put on death row. Antagonists just hours before, Patrick and Patterson were now on the same side. Within twenty-four hours, Patrick went from someone Patterson described as an out-and-out liar to the only one who knew the whole truth of what had occurred that night.

Stokes, who had advised Patrick not to take the stand in his own trial, had convinced him that now his only chance to avoid the electric chair was to help Patterson win a conviction against Archer. Patrick didn't know if this was true or not. He had never spoken to Patterson. But in his mind, this was his last, and only, chance to save his own life—even at the expense of another man's life.

Patrick's testimony would give Patterson the premeditation and money motives he needed to convict Archer of murder and make his case for the death penalty.

Patterson asked Patrick how the plan to rob Trout Auto came about. Patrick testified that Archer came over to his house with a briefcase full of money and said, "I want you to murder somebody."

Later in his testimony, Patrick told Patterson that he never received the briefcase full of money. The day after the murder, Archer came over to his house, Patrick testified, and taunted him for killing the wrong guy.

"He came up to me and he was kind of giggling and laughing and stuff and, you know, I kind of didn't even want him around me," Patrick said, "and he came up to me and was laughing, and he was all happy and he said, 'You killed the wrong man, no money for you,' and started laughing, you know."

When it was Archer's turn, his court-appointed attorney, E. Brian Lang, asked Patrick more about the briefcase full of money that he was supposed to receive for killing Wells. At the time, Lang reminded Patrick, Archer was staying with friends because he had no place to live and had been out of work for a year. And yet Patrick said Archer showed him a suitcase full of money.

Patrick knew Lang had him in a lie. The story of the briefcase was absurd, something a stupid kid would say. But, live or die, it was his story and there was no retreating now. The best he could do was hedge his answers.

"How much money was in that briefcase, Mr. Bonifay?" Lang asked.

"Don't know."

"You didn't ask how much money was in there?"

"He quoted $500,000, but there was no way," Patrick replied.

"Five hundred thousand?" Lang said.

"It had papers on it like it comes from a bank," Patrick said.

"Five hundred—a half a million dollars, is that what you're telling us?"

"He said that."

Lang asked if Patrick actually saw the money, and what it looked like: "Twenties, tens, hundreds, what?"

"Fifties," Patrick said.

"Fifties," Lang repeated. "Do you know how many bills are in a half million dollars of fifties?"

"No, sir."

Archer's trial, like Patrick's, lasted two days. The jury began deliberations at 3:15 P.M. on July 18 and reached a verdict at 5:30. As with Patrick, the verdict was sealed by the judge.

The verdicts were announced the following day, July 19, and they were identical for Patrick and Archer: guilty of first-degree murder, armed robbery, and grand theft.

The same day, Patterson presented his case to Patrick's jury that the boy deserved to die. Patrick's mother would try to convince them that he should live.

Life and Death 7

As she approached the witness stand in Judge Collier's courtroom, Theresa Crenshaw felt torn between a mother's shame that Patrick had taken another man's life and a mother's instinct to save her only child. But if she persuaded the jury to spare her seventeen-year-old son the death penalty, she risked indicting herself as the failed mother of a teenage killer. In Pensacola, she was the woman who gave birth to a monster. His guilt was hers also.

She felt revolted by how her son had cocked that gun, held it to Coker's head, and pulled the trigger twice. How could she make the jury understand what went on inside Patrick when she hardly knew herself? There was so much she didn't understand about her son.

Theresa was fifteen when she ran away from a strict father and met handsome, long-haired James Bonifay, an illiterate mechanic who would rather drink than work. She was too young to know herself any better than she knew her husband. The trouble between her and James started almost the minute she became pregnant. James became suicidal a month into the marriage, and then, while she was still pregnant, he shot off two of his toes—just to see if she cared. Patrick was born the day after Christmas in 1973. He seemed to emerge from her womb demanding things she couldn't give him. As a baby, he was sickly and hyperactive. Milk made him ill. He developed severe allergies and caught pneumonia five or six times before he was a year old. He started walking at nine months, and once he started talking he never stopped. It drove James nuts. Patrick just seemed to ignite his father's short fuse. James was rough with Patrick when they played together, and violent when Patrick misbehaved.

Theresa, nervous and anxious, needed tranquilizers and antidepressants to handle the daily stress and conflict in her life. Her confusion over what to do with Patrick began as soon as he started school. Patrick's kindergarten teacher made urgent requests for meetings with his parents. He's not following directions. He doesn't display good manners. He doesn't demonstrate self-control. He can't use time wisely. He doesn't keep his hands to himself. He won't eat his lunch. He won't participate in music. He cuts in line. He talks talks talks.

Patrick's fourth-grade teacher scribbled a plea at the end of his report card: "I think we need to schedule a conference for Patrick *as soon as possible*." But when they met, the teacher told Theresa, "I don't want your son in my class."

To Theresa, this sounded like a teacher shirking her responsibility. Patrick was entitled to an education. He needed help. *She* needed help. But the teachers seemed no better equipped to handle Patrick than Theresa was. They tried rewards, they tried punishments. Everything that seemed to work was followed by failure.

Patrick's main interaction with other kids was to wrestle and fight. At home, Patrick played too rough with his younger sister, Jody, who was as thin and meek as Patrick was big and aggressive.

At school, whatever friends Patrick made, he lost fighting. He was sensitive about kids touching his books, his toys, his clothes. When another kid snatched a pencil out of his pocket, Patrick picked up a chair and hit him.

Theresa didn't know what to do. When she tried to talk to him, he had no explanation except to say he didn't mean to.

Patrick seemed immune to discipline, indifferent to rewards, impervious to pain. He could step on a nail and not cry.

His demands grew louder as he grew older. Patrick wanted the expensive tennis shoes she couldn't afford. The cheap ones she bought him, he cut up.

His emotions were a light switch that could flip instantly from light to dark.

As she walked to the stand, Theresa had no delusions about what Patrick had done. He killed Coker, and she felt Patrick deserved to be in prison, maybe for the rest of his life. But she didn't want him to be executed. She wanted the jury to know, Yes, he's my son, but I didn't give birth to a monster. He is not the cold-blooded, Charlie Manson–like character he's been portrayed as in court. He's a kid, just a kid. He's my son.

Theresa braced herself to spill before the jury all the intimate secrets and embarrassments of her family. She had never been in a courtroom before, had never sat in the witness stand or faced a jury. Ted Stokes hadn't rehearsed her testimony beforehand, hadn't told her what he would be asking her, hadn't coached her on what to expect from Patterson. The only advice she got came from relatives, who told her to stay calm. Stay calm? she replied. They're trying to kill my kid! Anxious and scared, she sat in the witness stand to save her son's life, but the one thing foremost in her mind was *I don't want to throw up.*

Stokes asked her about her first husband, James Bonifay. Theresa testified to how James was violent toward her and Patrick.

"Did you become aware of some sexual abuse occurring between Patrick's natural father and Patrick?" Stokes asked.

"Yes, I did."

"And how old was Patrick when you became aware of that?"

Hesitantly, Theresa recounted how Patrick was about eleven or twelve when they were watching a movie together on TV about a child sexually molested by a parent. Patrick became emotional and upset. When she questioned him, he told her about what his father had done to him.

Stokes turned the subject to Patrick and his troubles in school.

"I asked them to test him in the third grade because they kept sending him home because he wouldn't do anything," Theresa testified. "And I told them that if he was retarded, I wanted him put in a special school. So they tested him and told me that no, he was not retarded, that he was emotionally disturbed and needed to be put in special ed."

In fifth grade, she explained, Patrick was enrolled in special-education classes for children with emotional disabilities. He was diagnosed with attention deficit disorder and placed on Ritalin.

"He couldn't sit down. He was very hyper, you know, jumping around and couldn't seem to concentrate on what he was doing," Theresa told the jury.

Stokes asked her if she believed that the boy she just described—this troubled, difficult adolescent, rejected by his teachers and abused by his family—could be "rehabilitated and be a productive member of society?"

In a steady, forceful voice, Theresa replied: "Yes, I do."

When it was his turn, Patterson homed in on Theresa's contention that Patrick was worth saving. He asked if she knew of all the bad things Patrick had done, if she knew about his involvement in the burglary of an auto-repair shop in Mississippi and that someone had been stabbed.

Yes, she replied, she knew what her son had done.

"And you still think he can be rehabilitated?" Patterson asked.

"Yes, I do," Theresa said.

"Is there anything your son could do that would make you believe he couldn't be rehabilitated?" he asked.

"No," Theresa replied. There was certainty, and defiance, in her voice.

Under Patterson's questioning, frustration began to replace the queasiness that had accompanied Theresa to the stand. Everything she said, or tried to say, was being twisted by the prosecutor. She knew what Patterson was doing: discrediting her and all she had told the jury about the difficulties in Patrick's life. *Don't believe her*, he was implying, *she's his mother*. When she stepped down from the witness stand, Theresa was no longer nervous and uncertain. She was angry.

Patterson had badgered her, made her feel like a liar, as if loving her son was a crime in itself. The conviction she had taken to the stand—that if she just spoke honestly, the jury would understand—was in ruins.

Theresa was asked to wait outside while Patrick testified. She had left the courtroom during the trial when they played Patrick's recorded statement to O'Neal, and now she would sit alone again, spared Patrick's recounting of what happened the night he killed Coker.

. . .

From his seat next to Stokes, Patrick listened to his mother's testimony just as he had listened to Cliff's. This wasn't his mother up there, speaking her true feelings. She was saying what Stokes wanted her to say. Any hope he had that his mother might be able to convince the jury that he was not something subhuman and evil had vanished.

Patrick hadn't expected his mother to tell this roomful of strangers the truth about how she whipped him with a garden hose. How she cared more about her china cabinet full of flea-market knickknacks than she did about him. How she'd leave him and Jody in the trailer alone for hours while she went and did her thing. How she was always threatening to send him back to his grandfather if he didn't behave.

If the jury was to hear the truth, the real truth, about his life, it would have to come from him.

. . .

When it was his turn on the stand, Patrick felt he could show the jury he didn't just crawl out of the Escambia swamps one day to terrorize Pensacola. He was here now because nobody wanted anything to do with him. His mother kicked him out. His teachers didn't want him in their classes. He grew up in a drug-infested rat hole. That's what the jury needed to know. He was not the devil who carefully calculated the robbery and murder of Billy Wayne Coker.

But on the stand, facing the jury, Patrick was subdued, his voice low, his words muffled by his hands. He was dressed in jeans and a long-sleeve hooded shirt. No dress shirt, no tie. He looked like he had walked off the street and straight to the witness stand. The courage he had summoned to commit the murder abandoned him in the courtroom.

"Did you want to kill the man?" Stokes asked him.

"No, sir."

"Are you sorry that you did?"

"Yes."

Stokes asked Patrick about James Bonifay's abusive behavior.

"You just heard your mother testify about some abuse that you received from your natural father when you were a child. Can you tell the jury about that?"

"My dad would just get mad and hit me."

"Where would he hit you, Patrick?"

"In the face and the head and all over," he said.

This public undressing of his childhood was difficult and embarrassing for Patrick. He wanted the truth told, but the questions Stokes asked were so personal and intimate. Stokes had done little to prepare him for this moment when his life was on the line. He was taking Patrick places he didn't want to go.

"I know that's a hard thing for you to talk about," Stokes said. "Can you tell the jury as best you can what sexual abuse took place?"

"No," Patrick replied. "He just—you know, he would mess with me and stuff."

"Was there oral sex?" Stokes asked.

"He did that to me."

"And how old were you then?"

"Young, eight or nine."

Before it was Patterson's turn to question Patrick, Stokes asked him about bouncing back and forth between his grandfather's house and his mother's trailer.

"Just like, you know, I go for a year, I'm at my mom's and then I'm back at my grandfather's and back over here and back over there," he said. "Just like they would put up with me as long as they could, and when they got tired of me, they would send me to somewhere else."

• • •

Patterson listened to Patrick's testimony, his mother's before that, and that of a clinical psychologist from Lakeview Center, a mental health facility in Pensacola. Patterson had read the psychological evaluation of Patrick when he was examined at Lakeview in 1985 for his disruptive behavior in school. Patrick, then eleven years old and in sixth grade, was described as a chubby kid with uncombed hair. A doctor had told Patrick he was so overweight that he couldn't hear his heartbeat. Patrick said he felt fat and stupid. He had no best friends. All the girls hated him. He told the psychologist he got angry when he was blamed for things, when someone tattled on him, or when he was accused of lying, and that his parents threatened him that "You better shut up while you can." The best thing he could say about himself was that he was good at video games and watching TV. If he had three wishes, he told the counselor, he'd want to have $10 million, live with his mother, and go fishing with his stepfather.

Patterson had read the report and thought, here's a kid who has spent his life blaming other people for his problems: Nobody loves me. Patrick always feels sorry for Patrick. Patterson was going to make sure nobody on the jury felt sorry for Patrick.

To build his case that Patrick was a teenage criminal who deserved the ultimate penalty for this murder, Patterson needed to peel away any sympathy the jury might have for Patrick the victim. Any hope Patrick had that testifying against Archer might put him on Patterson's good side vanished when it was the prosecutor's turn to question him about his childhood.

Patterson had heard the sexual-abuse, abusive-father defense before. It was becoming popular with defense attorneys, but those cases often had documented evidence of the severity and duration of the abuse. Patrick had none of that. Patterson had doubts of whether the molestation had happened at all or had contributed anything to Patrick's inclination to kill.

"You told your mother that you had been sexually abused by your father to get out of trouble, didn't you?" Patterson said. "And she took you seriously and took you to Lakeview, isn't that what happened? And when you got there, you said, whoops, better shave it down a little bit, isn't that what happened?"

"No."

"Did you ever talk to the police about this sexual abuse?"

"No."

"Never did," Patterson said. "Did Lakeview ever say, 'He's telling us about a serious crime, we better call the police and let them talk to him?'"

"Don't recall," Patrick replied.

"Never happened," Patterson said. "That's because you didn't tell the people at Lakeview about it, did you?"

"Yes, I did."

"What did you tell them?"

"Told them my dad had been messing with me."

Patterson then led Patrick through Coker's murder. Everywhere Stokes emphasized Archer's influence over Patrick, Patterson emphasized Patrick's influence over Cliff and Eddie. He wanted the jury to remember that it was Patrick who made all the decisions.

"Who was the leader?" he asked Patrick.

"There was no leader."

"There wasn't a leader," Patterson repeated. "You don't want to claim to be the leader now, do you?"

"Never did," Patrick replied.

"I see. Who told the other two about the plan?"

"I did."

"I see. Who got the gun?"

"I did."

"Who got the bolt cutters?"

"I did."

"I see. But you weren't the leader?"

Patrick shook his head no.

Patterson pressed him again: Who told Eddie where to park and told Cliff how to get in and get out of the store? Patrick answered that he did.

"But you weren't the leader?" Patterson said.

"They were just helping me," Patrick replied.

"Pardon me?"

"They were involved in it, too," Patrick said.

Patterson then attacked Stokes's assertion that Patrick was sorry for what he had done. Patterson saw no evidence of remorse, only the criminal misgiving of getting caught. If there were true remorse, Patrick would express his sorrow for the loss of Coker's life and the pain that his murder had inflicted upon Coker's wife and children.

"Isn't it true the only thing you're sorry about is that you got caught?"

"No, sir."

"You are sorry you got caught, aren't you?"

"No."

"You're not?" Patterson replied. "You're glad you got caught?"

"In a way."

His answers confirmed in Patterson's mind that Patrick was just saying what he thought he was supposed to say. The honest-to-God answer would have been, "Yes, I'm sorry I got caught, but I'm also sorry for what I did and the misery I've inflicted on the victim, his family, and my own family." Patrick had failed to deliver.

After reestablishing Patrick's belief that Archer was going to pay him to kill someone, Patterson revisited witnesses' testimony that Patrick had boasted about the killing to his friends. He didn't want the jury to forget that this teenager was a heartless killer.

"You were kind of anxious to kill somebody, weren't you?" Patterson said.

"No, sir."

"Didn't you brag that 'I'm ready to kill somebody. I want to see what it's like'?"

"No, sir."

"Never told anybody that?"

"No, sir."

Patterson focused on the moment Patrick killed Coker.

"And what did you do? Did you put the gun to the man's head?"

"Yes."

"Put it right next to his head?"

Patrick nodded.

"And you fired?"

In a voice barely audible, Patrick admitted he pulled the trigger but that he looked away when he pulled the trigger.

"Why did you turn away?"

"Because I was killing somebody."

"Why did you turn away?" Patterson insisted.

The switch between sorrow and anger clicked inside Patrick. He glared at Patterson.

"What am I supposed to do, just sit there and look at it?"

Patterson knew he had him. He broke through the self-pity that, to the jury, might look like remorse. He asked again, a taunt as much as a question: "Why did you turn away?"

"Because I didn't want to do it."

"You didn't want to do it," Patterson repeated. "Somebody was making you do it. You're not really responsible for what happened, are you?"

"Yes."

"You ought to get out of it because you were sexually abused when you were a child?" Patterson pressed. "And because your father wasn't nice to you or your stepfather wasn't nice to you, you ought to get out of this, isn't that what you are trying to tell this jury?"

"No," Patrick replied. "Only thing I'm saying is I know I did what I did. I just want them to know why."

All of Patrick's plans to get on the stand and make the jury understand the circumstances of his life were wadded up in Patterson's hands and tossed in his face.

"Know why?" asked Patterson.

Patrick nodded.

"And the reason is Robin Archer made you do it?"

"He told me he was going to hurt my family if I didn't."

Wasn't this the same Robin Archer who lived with your mother in the trailer behind his grandfather's business? asked Patterson. The same guy who lived with you and your mother threatened to kill her if you didn't do what he said.

Yes, answered Patrick. "People like Robbie don't care about nobody."

That afternoon, Patterson made his case to the jury that Patrick was the person who didn't care about anyone except himself.

"We have the defendant's mom and the defendant saying, 'Yes, I was terribly abused, so excuse me.' If you don't buy that reason, we have the other reason, 'Robin Archer, this horrible sinister person who made me do this. Robin Archer made me do it,'" Patterson said.

And then he concluded that if any killing of a human being cried out for the death penalty, it was Patrick's murder of Coker. "There could not be a more horrible premeditated, cruel, wicked thing to do to a person than to walk up to them while they are hurt and bleeding and lying on the floor begging for their family and then casually put a gun to their head and kill them," he said.

In his last chance to save Patrick's life, Stokes asked the jury to take a good look at Patrick and see him for who he really was: a teenager, a stupid, impulsive teenager. Stokes made a final attempt to separate the juvenile from the act that made him an adult. He reminded the jury that Patrick was not a fully formed, mature grown-up. This was not a well-plotted, carefully crafted crime, but a senseless, irrational crime by a desperate boy under the influence of an older man.

"Nobody has come in here and told you that this was any brilliant thing to do," he said. "It certainly was a dumb thing to do. It was a juvenile thing to do. And I would submit to you that that's why Robin Archer had these kids do it, because he knew better. He was older. He had better sense than to go out and do something like this. These kids didn't think through what they were going to do. They didn't think about the consequences."

Patrick, Stokes told the jury, was a teenager who missed out on the things a youngster needs in growing up: stability, love, guidance. Instead of giving him death, give him another chance at life.

"All I'm asking you to do is throw that lifeline to Patrick Bonifay," Stokes begged.

When it came time for the jury to deliberate, Judge Collier gave them the instructions that apply only in Florida. In other states, only a unanimous jury can sentence a person to death. In Florida, it takes a simple majority.

• • •

While the jury deliberated, Patrick waited alone in a large holding cell inside the courthouse. There were benches alongside the walls and one bench in the middle. The walls were tan and bare. A bailiff handed him a sack lunch with an orange inside. He sat on the bench by the door. On the stand he had kept his eyes on Patterson, who walked back and forth while questioning him. *The prick. What an asshole*, Patrick had thought. Patrick didn't look at the jury. He didn't need to. He could imagine what they were thinking. If it were him in that jury box, he would probably be thinking the same thing.

In about the time it took Patrick to eat his orange, the jury made up its mind.

. . .

As the jury filed into the courtroom on Friday afternoon, July 19, the foreman handed Judge Collier the piece of paper that contained their decision. Ten to two, the jury recommended the death penalty for Patrick Bonifay.

Patrick exhaled, his head dropped to his chest, tears filled his eyes. As he cried, Stokes put an arm around him.

Patrick's mother felt the sick and brokenhearted confirmation of what she knew was surely coming. But there was also an unexpected sense of relief: It's over, it's done. At last, the nightmare is ending.

That same day, Archer's jury deliberated for seventy-nine minutes. They came back with a seven-to-five vote for the death penalty, one vote shy of giving Archer a life sentence.

Patterson's job was half done. The following month he would prosecute Cliff and Eddie.

. . .

On August 26, 1991, juries for the trials of Eddie and Cliff were selected from the same pool of jurors. To Eddie's attorney, Elton Killam, the whole thing looked staged, a crafty choreography by Patterson to make Eddie's jury believe that Cliff was facing the same possibility of life, or death, as Eddie. There was no question in Killam's mind that Cliff was not going to stand trial. He was going to testify as a state's witness against Eddie, just as he had against Patrick and Archer. In return, Cliff would avoid going to court and death row. For his contention that Cliff's jury selection was a farce, Killam was threatened with contempt of court by Judge Collier.

If Killam was sure that Cliff was not going to trial, Cliff was just as certain that he was. Even as he prepared to testify against Eddie, Cliff was anticipating his own trial. He believed the jury would find him innocent. In his mind, justice was as simple as the basic fact that he hadn't killed anyone.

Cliff's lawyer, Michael Allen, didn't want to risk a trial. He understood what Cliff couldn't comprehend, that in Florida, felony murder applies to anyone involved in a crime that results in a murder. You don't need to be the one who planned it; you don't need to be the one who pulled the trigger. Florida prisons are full of people who were in the wrong place, at the wrong time, with the wrong person.

In early July, in a four-page letter to Cliff, Allen had laid out how unrealistic Cliff's thinking was. In point-blank language, he explained the slim chance that a jury would find Cliff innocent. By going to trial, Cliff risked either the death penalty or two consecutive life sentences.

Allen urged Cliff to plead guilty to the murder and robbery. Cliff refused. He believed he had an agreement with Patterson. And he had held up his end of the deal. It was *his* testimony that helped put Patrick on death row, *his* testimony that helped convict Archer. And *his* testimony would help Patterson win his case against Eddie. In return, Patterson would spare his life. Isn't that how it's supposed to work? But here was his lawyer telling him he was headed to death row if he didn't plead guilty to a murder he didn't commit. He kept telling Allen, "I didn't kill anybody," and it was like his attorney wasn't even listening—like it doesn't even matter whether he did or he didn't. It was just crazy. The prosecutor was telling him one thing, his own attorney was telling him the opposite. He trusted Patterson more than he trusted Allen. He wanted his trial. He wanted his day in court.

The night before his trial, Cliff met with his attorney. They didn't go over what to expect the next day, the defense strategy, or Cliff's testimony. Allen talked to Cliff about the death penalty and what it's like on death row, what a young kid like him could expect. Shaken and confused, Cliff still insisted he wanted to go to trial.

On the morning of August 27, wearing a new brown suit and a new pair of shoes his parents bought for his trial, Cliff was led to a small room off the courtroom. He had been expecting to see his parents seated in the courtroom gallery. He wasn't expecting to talk to them, but there they were in the small room where Allen said he was going to give them a few minutes alone, and then closed the door. Cliff didn't know what to do or say. His parents sat across the table from him, crying about the death penalty and pleading with him to plea-bargain for the sake of his life and theirs. He didn't understand their fears.

"Mom, Dad, I didn't kill anyone," he told them. "Even if they convict me, they're not going to give me the death penalty—the prosecutor told me so. I helped Patterson get two convictions."

But Cliff's parents kept insisting that's not what his lawyer said. He said you're going to get convicted and you're going to die, they warned. Cliff felt torn between what he wanted to do and what his parents were telling him to do. They were crying, and it made him cry, too. The tears and debate went on for forty-five minutes. Just before his trial was to start, Cliff gave in.

In the courtroom, Patterson and Allen stood together before Judge Collier.

"Your honor, I've discussed this matter with my client, Cliff Barth. Cliff is, of course, a juvenile," Allen said. "I've also talked with his parents and we've met together, talked together with Cliff, and they've had an opportunity to talk to him alone. It's my understanding that if Cliff wants to change his plea, that the State would not seek a death penalty if he pleads to a first-degree murder charge, and the State would recommend that on the robbery charge there be a term of years to run concurrent with the life sentence on the first-degree murder charge. And with that understanding, Cliff and his parents have expressed to me that he wants to change his plea to a plea of guilty rather than to go ahead and have a trial in this case."

A few minutes later, Cliff stood before Judge Collier in his stiff new suit, answering "Yes, sir" to every question. But his mind was somewhere else. He had just agreed to plead guilty to a murder he did not commit. A feeling of unreality again swept through him. *This can't be happening. I don't believe it. This isn't real.*

"How old are you, Mr. Barth?" Collier said.

"Seventeen."

"And what has been your educational experience?" the judge asked.

"I got arrested when I was in the eleventh grade," Cliff replied.

"Your education, how far have you been in school?" Collier repeated.

"Completed tenth grade," Cliff said.

"Alright," Collier said. "And what have you been doing—did you drop out of school or did this interfere with the school or what?"

"I got arrested while I was in school."

"And how did you do in school?" Collier asked.

"Average."

Sandra Coker was in the courtroom listening to the exchange between the judge and Cliff. Patterson addressed the judge.

"Your honor," he said, "before we conclude the proceedings, Mrs. Coker, the victim's widow, is present and this morning I discussed the possibility of not seeking the death penalty against Mr. Barth, and Mrs. Coker this morning communicated to me that that was acceptable to her. Is that correct, Mrs. Coker?"

"That's right," Sandra Coker replied.

Cliff's plea completed, Collier asked the teen again if he had anything else to say.

"No, sir," he replied.

"Alright," Collier said. "Are we ready to proceed in the case of the State vs. Larry Fordham Jr.?"

Cliff's appearance before Judge Collier was more a dress rehearsal than an actual plea. Patterson wanted to wait until after Eddie's trial to formally enter Cliff's guilty plea. If Cliff should change his mind, his jury was still waiting in the wings. The prosecutor wasn't taking any chances. He wanted Cliff to testify against Eddie before he signed off on any plea bargain. He didn't have long to wait. That same day, Cliff took the stand against Eddie. His testimony was damning.

Facing Eddie, who was seated at the defendant's table dressed in a suit coat, white shirt, and maroon paisley tie, Cliff described Eddie's role in the robbery and Coker's murder: Eddie was there when Patrick was talking about robbing Trout Auto; Eddie supplied the ski mask to Patrick; Eddie helped to buy the bullets; Eddie sat beside Patrick as he loaded the gun; and Eddie, after the robbery when they were dividing up the money, exclaimed, "Who says crime doesn't pay?"

• • •

What Cliff told the jury was bad, but to Eddie's thinking it was more damaging to Cliff than it was to him. Cliff had changed his story from his earlier testimony, and Eddie could prove it. He assembled it all for Killam: Cliff's statement in Patrick's trial was different from what he said at Archer's trial, and now he told a different version at Eddie's trial. Killam could show the jury how Cliff lied under oath. He'd be exposed as a witness without credibility.

Eddie was eager, also, for his chance to get on the stand. The jury needed to hear his story from his lips. He was on trial for murder, but it should be for ignorance. His only crime was being naive.

Under questioning by Killam, Eddie tried to appear confident as he told the jury how Patrick had deliberately kept him in the dark as they sat in Eddie's truck outside Trout Auto Parts that Saturday night.

But as he was finally getting the chance to tell the jury—to tell the world—the true story of his involvement in Trout Auto, he was feeling nervous, anxious, and uncertain. Killam hadn't rehearsed his testimony with him before he took the stand. He hadn't given Eddie much direction at all. His only advice to Eddie was to look at the jury while he testified.

Eddie looked at the jury. There were seven men and six women. This jury of his peers was old enough to be his parents. As he was telling them the story he had been dying to tell for six months, even as the words were coming out of his mouth, he was thinking, *They don't believe me.*

Under cross-examination by Patterson, Eddie stuck to the story he told Patterson the day they met inside the Escambia County Jail. In the most assured voice he could aim at the jury, he reiterated that he didn't know there was going to be a robbery at Trout Auto and that a man was going to be killed. He insisted to the jury what he had maintained all along: He thought they were at Trout Auto for a drug deal.

If Patterson appeared intimidating in that small interview room inside the jail, in the open expanse of the courtroom he looked invincible. To Eddie, he looked like Superman in an expensive suit.

So you're not guilty of anything, Patterson said after Eddie had finished.

"I'm guilty of not thinking," Eddie answered.

Patterson wanted the jury to see Eddie not as the naive, easily manipulated kid controlled and influenced by Patrick Bonifay but as a teenager who made his own choices. He asked Eddie whether he spent his money from the robbery at the Cordova Mall the next day. Eddie said yes. He bought a $140 wet suit because Patrick told him he'd better spend the money or there would be "complications."

"He threatened you," Patterson said. "'You better enjoy this money or there will be trouble.' Is that what he said?"

"Somewhat," Eddie answered, "but I didn't enjoy it."

When it was Killam's turn again on redirect, he asked Eddie about talking with Patterson in the county jail about testifying against Patrick and Cliff.

"And the reason you didn't testify against these other people is because you didn't tell Mr. Patterson what he wanted to hear, is that right?"

"Mr. Patterson said, 'Tell me what I want to hear,'" Eddie replied.

"He wasn't happy with you, was he?" Killam asked.

"No. He stormed out of the room."

When it was Patterson's turn again, he was still not happy. Eddie remained the kid who thought he could talk his way out of jam. Patterson thought this was his chance to take control of his story. He went right at Eddie.

"In their trials, why did I not want you to testify?" asked Patterson.

"Because I was going to tell the truth," Eddie replied. If Patterson was going to push, Eddie would push back.

"Is that what I said—I don't want you to testify because you're going to tell the truth?"

"No, sir, that is not."

"What did I say?"

"You said, 'Eddie, you have not even begun to meet me halfway yet,'" Eddie said.

"Mr. Fordham, didn't I say you're lying about your involvement and I won't put a witness on the stand that is going to lie about any part of it?"

In the give-and-take of the courtroom, Eddie knew that Patterson was shoving him around. He turned his face away from the jury and stifled the urge to cry.

Patterson took one last shot at Eddie's facade of control. Killam had questioned Cliff about his contradictory testimony, which Eddie himself had pointed out to Killam. Patterson could see on Eddie's face the smug look of points scored in a game of gotcha!

When Eddie made the point that in each trial Cliff implicated someone else, Patterson pointed out that Patrick did the same thing.

"Yes, he did, but I'm sure yesterday's testimony cross-examination of Mr. Barth will prove that he wasn't a very good witness," Eddie said, regaining some of his composure.

"You were pretty excited about that, weren't you?" Patterson said.

"Yes, because the truth came out," Eddied responded.

Patterson then deliberately stepped over the line, raising an immediate objection from Killam.

"As a matter of fact," Patterson said to Eddie, "I think you told someone 'I'm going to beat this case,' didn't you?"

Killam said he was going to ask for a mistrial, and Patterson withdrew the question.

By midafternoon that day, August 28, Eddie's future was in the hands of the jury. As they deliberated for three and a half hours, Eddie awaited their verdict alone in a holding cell. He thought about all he had missed the past eight months while his friends and classmates celebrated the boys' baseball team winning the state championship and posed for photographs in their blue-and-orange graduation caps and gowns. Less than a year ago, when a student at Escambia High had shot another kid to death at a birthday party, Eddie condemned the teenager. He should get the death penalty, he told everyone. They should fry him. Now it was Eddie waiting for a jury to pass judgment on him, and wondering if they would decide the same about him: This boy should fry.

Alone in the room, he cried, he prayed, he shouted at the walls, until he heard the bailiff's footsteps coming down the hall and the keys at the door.

"They're ready for you, Mr. Fordham."

Eddie nodded, took a deep breath, and followed the bailiff into the courtroom, where everyone except the jury awaited him. He tried to read their faces as they filed in, one by one, and took their seats. They looked tired and ready to go home. He hoped they were ready to send him home as well. After all this was over, he thought, if his parents wanted to put him on a long, long restriction, that would be okay with him.

The jury foreman rose and announced the verdict: guilty of grand theft, armed robbery with a firearm, and felony murder. The felony murder conviction sent a jolt through Eddie. He knew Patterson could now seek the death penalty.

Diana Fordham cried out in the courtroom. Larry Fordham shouted, "Son, it's not over yet."

The next day, Patterson stood before the judge and said that because Eddie was not present when Patrick murdered Coker, he would not seek the death penalty for Eddie.

Eddied was stunned and relieved, but confused. He turned to his lawyer.

"He doesn't think he can convince the jury to recommend the death sentence against you," Killam said.

Eddie's future, like Cliff's and Patrick's, was now known. No high school graduation. No military service. No weddings. They were all going to prison. The only thing that remained unknown was for how long and where. The following month, they would receive their sentences.

. . .

On September 18, Eddie Fordham stood before Judge Collier for sentencing. Eddie, the wheelman who wouldn't flip, received a life sentence for the felony murder conviction, seventy-five years for the robbery, and five years for grand theft—all to be served concurrently. He would be eligible for parole in twenty-five years.

A tearful Eddie told the judge, "All my dreams have been destroyed." As he was led from the courtroom, Eddie waved to family members and, to his crying mother, touched his face in a gesture that encouraged her to keep her chin up.

At his sentencing, Cliff stood stoically between his parents, his father's hand resting on his shoulder, as Patterson and Judge Collier praised him for his cooperation—for acting like an adult.

"Your honor, I would ask the court to give Mr. Barth every consideration that the court is empowered by law to give. He, of all of the individuals involved in this, he alone initially, and with great feeling, expressed remorse and concern for the Coker family from the outset," Patterson said. "His willingness to be forthright and truthful in this matter was the only piece of goodness that came out of any of the defendants involved in this case."

The judge agreed: "Well, I do want to state for the record that I always have been impressed with the conduct of Mr. Barth despite the fact of his participation in these matters which is, of course, deserving of punishment. But his conduct since then has been distinctly different from any of the others that participated in this matter. As you point out, he has acknowledged his participation and acceptance of blame, has not attempted to minimize it in this court's opinion. And while his participation was perhaps even more so than others, it is clear to me from having observed him during three trials and during these proceedings, that he is truly a follower rather than a leader, probably particularly related to his age, and lacks the sophistication that some of the other participants have in this case."

As he had with Eddie, Collier sentenced Cliff to life for the felony murder. But with Cliff, who held the gun on Coker, the judge reduced the armed-robbery charge to robbery without a weapon. Instead of the seventy-five years Eddie received, Cliff was sentenced to five years. Collier gave him another five years for petty theft, both sentences to run alongside his life sentence. Like Eddie, Cliff would be eligible for parole after twenty-five years.

Listening to Judge Collier pronounce his sentence, Cliff experienced a moment of lucidity, a parting of the out-of-body sense of disbelief that had engulfed him from the moment he slid out of Eddie's truck outside Trout Auto. *This is real. This is really happening. My life is over.*

The next day, the *Pensacola News Journal* published a letter from Eddie to Patrick and Cliff—the first of many in which he blamed his imprisonment on false friends: "Thanks a lot, you so-called friends of mine. You said 'Eddie, we'll always be together, no matter what.' But I never thought we'd be together in prison for the next 25 years . . . You've drained me of my family, my career, my girlfriend, and most of all my freedom. I'm only 18 years old and I'll be 43 before I ever see my family again . . . You should have just as well used the other bullets on me, because you've killed so much around me. You've taken my life . . ."

On September 20, Judge Collier formally sentenced Patrick to death for the murder, to life for the armed robbery, and to five years for grand theft. The sentences were to run consecutively. If he survived death row, Patrick would begin his life sentence for the robbery.

"Nothing could be more heinous, atrocious and cruel than the termination of an already severely wounded husband and father as he pled for his life," Collier said. "Nothing could be more torturous than to beg for mercy in the name of one's wife and children and to die with the killer cursing their existence. . . . This is the classic case of murder for hire, contract murder and execution."

Archer received the same sentence—death and then life. Archer stared straight at the judge as he was sentenced to death, then turned to look at his family, and grinned.

There had been death threats against Collier and Patterson, and the courtroom was thick with armed officers. A couple of them blocked Archer's father, William Archer, when he tried to approach his son after sentencing. While being escorted from the courtroom, William Archer said to Patterson, "I hope bad things happen to your family . . . I hope you burn in hell."

Five days later, Patrick, Eddie, Cliff, and Archer boarded a prison transport van at the county jail for the five-hour ride from Pensacola to the Lake Butler Reception and Medical Center. Toward the front of the van, Eddie was shackled to Cliff, whose testimony had contributed to his murder conviction. In the back, Archer was handcuffed to Patrick, whose testimony had landed both of them on death row. None of the four had been in prison before. All rode in silence, deep in their thoughts of the life receding behind them and the uncertainty of what lay ahead.

They had all heard the stories from the old-timers in the county jail about what to expect from the "Lake Butler Experience." The House of Pain had a reputation for brutality, the correctional officers like sadistic drill sergeants at the Parris Island of the prison system. The guards will attack you, unprovoked, get you down, and kick your teeth out. They have a jar filled with the gold teeth of prisoners they brutalized.

It was raining for much of the ride. In the back of the van, Patrick tried to prepare himself mentally for his immediate transfer from Lake Butler to Florida State Prison in Starke. *Death row, what is that like? I got to be ready to defend myself. If somebody comes at me, what do I do?*

Death Row 8

To Patrick, death row felt like a slaughterhouse. The prison reeked with the smell, the aura, of the condemned. It was late on the night he arrived, September 25, 1991, and Patrick felt exhausted from the long day and bumpy ride from Lake Butler to Starke. The chains draping his orange prison uniform hung heavy, and the shackles gnawed at his ankles. Guards led him down a darkened catwalk toward his cell on R Wing. The light from a few cells spilled through the bars, softly illuminating the peeling paint and broken windows on the outer wall. The old prison looked antiquated and obsolete, reminding Patrick of the dungeons he had seen on TV and in the movies. All the sounds seemed amplified. He flinched like a cat at the loud bang and clank of doors slamming shut, locks clicking, wheels turning.

The guards stopped him at Cell 3. He looked through the bars at the mess inside. Dirty, disgusting. The cell door clanged open; he stepped inside and it banged shut, scattering cockroaches across the floor. Flecks of paint fell from the ceiling. The floor was sticky. He backed against the cell door so the guards could unlock his shackles and handcuffs.

Alone, Patrick looked around the six-by-nine cell. Roaches. Cigarette butts. A stainless-steel toilet in the corner. A steel sink. A mirror made of polished metal. A small TV on a ledge. The bed was a slab of metal protruding out from the wall, a thin mattress rolled up on one end. The cell was cold. The wing was quiet except for the audio from a couple of TV sets and the distant, unintelligible voices of men he could not see.

Patrick unrolled the mattress, climbed into bed, and fell right to sleep.

Morning came early. The predawn wake-up shook Patrick from his sleep. He swung his legs off the bunk. Outside his cell was a large paper bag. He pulled it though the bars and found it filled with snacks, coffee, paper, envelopes, a pen, and magazines contributed by the other inmates as they passed the sack from cell to cell. Inside the bag was a note welcoming him to death row.

Patrick asked for a broom and a mop. The cell's filth reminded him of the condemned men who came before him. He scrubbed the floor and washed the walls. The smell remained even after Patrick's cleaning, but his desire for neatness and order was satisfied.

The food disgusted him. Patrick pulled the plastic cafeteria tray through the slot in his cell door from the trustee who pushed the metal cart along R Wing. All the food was sloshed together. He couldn't get used to eating bread and cookies soaked in the juice of collard greens. Sometimes the meat was cold, sometimes raw. Patrick learned to peck through the food with his plastic spork for bits of grit and glass.

During the day, Patrick could hear the radios and TV sets from the other cells on the row. Men held conversations by shouting. They carried on legal arguments, talked politics and sports.

In the cell to his left was a man who called himself Bandit. The guy in the cell to the right was Jackhammer. Bandit was quiet, Jackhammer loud and sociable. Nobody had told Patrick what to expect from death row. It wasn't something that Ted Stokes talked to him about. It wasn't something the older prisoners in the county jail had experienced. Patrick asked the other guys the question that most bothered him since he received the death penalty.

"How long before they kill us?" Patrick asked.

"Man, you got a long time before you have to worry about that," Jackhammer replied.

There was no reason to ask other inmates what they were in for or how long they'd been there. Every man in every cell was a murderer. Every man was condemned. Every man was isolated from the others, released from his cell every other day for a quick shower and twice a week for four hours of exercise. It didn't take Patrick long to identify and avoid the areas of the yard outside the view of cameras where inmate sex took place.

The guards treated the death-row prisoners differently than the other men. They didn't try to provoke or intimidate them, assert their authority or demonstrate their toughness. There seemed to be something as close to a mutual understanding as there can be between guards and prisoners. The men behind the bars knew what everyone else wants to ignore: they are going to die. They not only knew that they would die, but also how and when. People outside the walls lived with the uncertainty of when their time would come, while each condemned man knew, at some point, the precise date and time of his death. That forbidden knowledge made them resigned or dangerous. Death-row guards had nothing to gain from antagonizing men who had nothing to lose except their mind. Other inmates feared for their safety; death-row prisoners feared for their sanity. The average death-row inmate in Florida spends twelve years awaiting execution—twelve years of isolation and confinement, twenty-three of every twenty-four hours spent alone in a prison cell, just thinking. Patrick noticed that some of the other prisoners talked to themselves as if thinking out loud, unaware that others could hear them. He wondered how long it would be until his hands started trembling and the voices in his head became too loud to ignore. He knew of those who killed themselves, or tried to, while waiting to be killed.

Patrick was a month into his death-row experience, trying to preserve his sanity by reading, writing letters, and watching TV, when Jerome Allen, a skinny black kid with big ears, moved into Cell 4. It was sometime in the afternoon, and through the bars of his cell Patrick could see that Jerome was about his size, but much younger.

Jerome was fifteen when he and two other teenagers were convicted of murdering a gas station attendant in Titusville on December 10, 1990. His case mirrored Patrick's—three teenagers involved in a robbery that resulted in a murder. But justice is seldom consistent and often arbitrary, especially in how juries of adults view the irrational, irresponsible actions of teenagers. In Jerome's case, seventeen-year-old Eugene Robertson, who pulled the trigger on the shotgun that killed Stephen DuMont, was sentenced to life in prison for the same act for which Patrick received the death penalty. Sixteen-year-old Brian Patrick Kennedy, who drove the car, did what Eddie Fordham refused to do—turned state's witness and received a life sentence in exchange for testifying that Eugene shot DuMont only after Jerome yelled at him to kill the man to prevent him from identifying them. Jerome Allen, who, like Clifford Barth, was inside the crime scene but never pulled the trigger, was sentenced to die.

Florida hadn't executed anyone as young as Jerome since 1941, but it remained one of eighteen states with no age limit for the death penalty. The state reflected the view of many people, including the families of Billy Wayne Coker and Stephen DuMont, that age was irrelevant when it came to murder. At Jerome's sentencing, the prosecutor argued that because Jerome killed like an adult, he deserved to die like an adult. Jerome became the youngest person condemned to death in the United States.

On death row, Jerome didn't behave like an adult when they closed the door to his cell on October 25, 1991. He and Patrick acted like they were back in elementary school. They tuned their TVs to *Scooby-Doo* and *Ninja Turtles* cartoons at seven in the morning. They laughed out loud. They talked about comic books and their G.I. Joes. They ate cookies and chips, made up batches of Tang, and got drunk together on prison-made wine. They engaged the trustee in water fights, the older inmate dousing them with buckets of water. Patrick and Jerome could hear the other prisoners griping and growling about all the noise and foolishness, turning death row into Romper Room, but nobody told them to knock it off and grow up.

Jerome's age became the basis for his appeal. Soon after his conviction, his attorneys filed an appeal contending that his death sentence violated Florida's Constitution, which prohibited cruel and unusual punishment.

Jerome's appeal came as a spasm of fear spread across Florida from a series of violent crimes committed by juveniles. This time a murder by a group of juveniles more than two hundred miles from Pensacola threatened the state's most important industry—tourism.

State of Alarm

Gary Colley pulled the Chevrolet Cavalier rental car into the parking space in the Interstate 10 rest stop near Monticello, Florida, at 1:30 A.M. on September 14, 1993. Colley, a thirty-four-year-old truck driver from Great Britain, and Margaret Ann Jagger, his thirty-five-year-old girlfriend, needed a nap for their nonstop drive from New Orleans to St. Petersburg. The couple had been coming to the United States every fall for fourteen years, but this time, instead of their usual four-week visit, they only had two weeks. They were in a hurry to get to St. Petersburg, where they planned to stay with friends.

Colley and Jagger had lived together for seven years in a cottage in the town of Wilsden in northern England. The couple loved to vacation in the United States, and particularly in Florida. They had even thought of moving to the States, but concerns over crime and violence held them back. Both of them hated guns.

The couple was aware of attacks on foreign tourists in recent months. In their New Orleans hotel room they watched a program about two German tourists who had been murdered five days earlier in Miami—the seventh and eighth tourists to be killed in the past year. They talked about how foolish those Germans had been, the mistakes they had made that led to their death.

The I-10 rest stop, about thirty miles east of Tallahassee, was nestled among giant oaks with long beards of Spanish moss, a stand of palms, and hedges of holly bushes. The air smelled faintly of pine. Several people were sleeping in their parked cars. Weary motorists walked in and out of restrooms built of brown brick with slanting corrugated metal roofs. A washroom attendant kept a watchful eye over the restrooms. The couple felt safe, and sleepy, as they closed their eyes in the front seats of their rental car.

Twenty minutes later, they were awoken by the tapping of a gun barrel on the passenger-side window. Jagger opened her eyes and looked into the face of a young black man. For a moment she thought how handsome he was, and in her half sleep she wondered what a good-looking kid like that was doing pointing a gun at her. He was yelling at her, but she couldn't hear what he was saying: "Give it up! Give it up!"

"I can't hear you," Jagger said to the boy outside the window. "I don't know what you want. What do you want?"

And then she realized, from the expression on his face, that the boy with the gun was going to shoot her, and she was going to die.

On the driver's side, next to Colley's window, stood another black youth with a gun. When Jagger glanced at him, he stepped away from the window and into the darkness.

Colley turned the key in the ignition and threw the car in reverse, backing into a red Pontiac Bonneville stolen earlier that night and containing two other black teens. As he tried to escape, four bullets were fired into the car, shattering the windows on both sides. In the explosion of splintered glass, Jagger felt the bullet pass through her right arm and graze her chest. It struck Colley in the neck. The .38-caliber bullet severed Colley's carotid artery, tore through a lung, and became embedded deep in his back. Jagger saw him flop forward, blood streaming from his neck, mouth, and nose. The blood filled Colley's chest, lungs, and throat. As Colley drowned in his own blood, the two gunmen ran back to the Bonneville and jumped inside.

The teenager who hopped into the front seat yelled at the driver to get moving: "Dip, man, dip!"

Outside the car they left behind, Jagger was screaming for help.

The report of Colley's murder at the I-10 rest stop shocked Florida in much the same way that Billy Wayne Coker's death in the wake of convenience store murders put Pensacola on edge. Governor Lawton Chiles ordered armed security at Florida's rest stops. The threat to the state's $31 billion tourist industry—and especially to its pipeline of British visitors—immediately became the top priority of the Florida Legislature, which was to meet six weeks later for a five-day special session.

The state had reason for concern that its major industry was under attack from within. As with the murders of the German tourists, Colley's death was worldwide news, the headlines of British papers screaming "Holiday of Horror" and "Come to Sunny Florida and Be Murdered for Absolutely Nothing."

When four black teenagers from Monticello—seventeen-year-old Deron Spear, sixteen-year-old John Crumitie, fourteen-year-old Aundra Akins, and thirteen-year-old Cedric Green—were arrested and charged with Colley's murder, Florida residents reacted much as the people of Pensacola had: juvenile crime was out of control.

Politicians responded to the public outcry. Although Crumitie and Akins were charged with shooting Colley to death, it was Green, sitting in the backseat of the car, who became the new face in Florida of the rising menace of teenage crime and the wrist-slapping juvenile justice system. Small and chubby-cheeked, Green had been arrested fifteen times on fifty-six charges before Colley's murder.

Cedric Green became Florida's Willie Bosket.

The special legislative session did little to address the public's concerns about juvenile crime except for making it illegal for juveniles to possess handguns and punishing those who did with community service and revoking the driver's licenses of kids often too young to drive anyway.

When legislators came back in February for the general session, they meant business. The 1994 Juvenile Justice Act expanded the "direct file" powers of prosecutors to send kids as young as fourteen into the adult criminal justice system, to permit juveniles to be sentenced to life without parole for crimes other than murder, and to try juveniles as adults, regardless of age, when they commit three felonies. The legislature also closed the last loophole in the parole system, eliminating parole for murder.

Giving prosecutors more authority to charge juveniles as adults vaulted Florida ahead of other states in this statistic. In 1995, Florida prosecutors charged seven thousand juveniles as adults—more than any other state, and nearly as many as the rest of the nation combined.

The state legislature also made a formal break from the turn-of-the-century Progressives' social-service approach to kids and crime by removing juvenile justice from the Florida Department of Health and Rehabilitative Services and creating a new Department of Juvenile Justice under the governor's office.

Legislators also continued the state's unprecedented expansion of the prison system by adding more than twenty-three thousand beds in two years, at a cost of $386 million—the equivalent of constructing from scratch a prison system larger than thirty-two other states'.

Florida was not alone in taking a hard line on juvenile crime. North Carolina also passed a law in 1995 allowing thirteen-year-olds to be tried as adults, joining New York, New Jersey, Louisiana, Tennessee, and South Carolina in making it easier to transfer the youngest teens into adult court.

Yet at the same time the politicians were enacting the public's perception that juvenile criminals were kids in age only, the courts were beginning to draw a distinction between youth and maturity. Instead of erasing the line between juvenile and adult, judges were beginning to draw a bright line of demarcation.

In Florida it was Jerome Allen, Patrick's death-row playmate, who changed the definition of who was and who wasn't old enough to be executed.

On March 24, 1994, around the time the Florida Legislature was enacting its get-tough reforms, the Florida Supreme Court ruled in *Jerome Allen v. the State of Florida* that the death penalty no longer applied to anyone younger than sixteen. The relevant argument, the justices said, wasn't that teenagers are too immature to deserve death, but rather that the penalty had become obsolete. Several teens as young as Jerome had been convicted of murder in the fifty years since Florida executed Willie Clay in 1941, but only three (including Jerome) had been sentenced to death. That fact alone made it unusual. Its arbitrary application made it cruel.

"We cannot countenance a rule that would result in some young juveniles being executed while the vast majority of others are not, even where the crimes are similar," the justices wrote.

The state supreme court revoked Jerome's death sentence and gave the teenager life in prison without any chance of parole for twenty-five years. Declaring him in essence a child, they made sure he wouldn't get out of prison until he reached middle age.

The court's ruling and the legislature's reaction to the tourist murders placed Florida directly on the fault line of debate taking place nationwide over the causes and consequences of violent teenage crime.

On one side were law-and-order conservatives led by political scientist John J. Dilulio Jr., who coined the term "super-predator" to describe the new breed of teenage criminal. Dilulio, a Princeton professor and director of the Brookings Institution Center for Public Management, laid out the case that inner-city moral poverty was multiplying the number of youths growing up without affection for or allegiance to anyone but themselves. Their brutality reflected childhoods devoid of love but abundant with unmerciful abuse, which they later revisited on their victims. He quantified the coming tidal wave of teenage violence with the finding that 6 percent of juvenile boys commit 50 percent of crimes. Given the population increase in teenagers, by the year 2000 the United States would have "30,000 more murderers, rapists, and muggers on the streets than we have today," Dilulio predicted in 1995.

"On the horizon, therefore, are tens of thousands of severely morally impoverished juvenile super-predators. They are perfectly capable of committing the most heinous acts of physical violence for the most trivial reasons. . . . They fear neither the stigma of arrest nor the pain of imprisonment. They live by the meanest code of the meanest streets, a code that reinforces rather than restrains their hairtrigger mentality," Dilulio argued. "So for as long as their youthful energies hold out, they will do what comes 'naturally': murder, rape, rob, assault, burglarize, deal deadly drugs and get high."

The United States, Dilulio wrote, was woefully unprepared for the coming deluge of this new breed of criminal. Between 1985 and 1991 the number of juveniles in jail had increased from 49,000 to nearly 58,000. "By my estimate, we will probably need to incarcerate at least 150,000 juvenile criminals in the years just ahead," he predicted. "In deference to public safety, we will have little choice but to pursue genuine get-tough law enforcement strategies against the super-predators."

Dilulio's case resonated with lawmakers across the country, including Florida's legislators. On the other side, researchers and child advocates were building an argument for understanding the mind, emotions, and behaviors of teenagers that found a forum in the courts.

Psychology professor Terrie E. Moffitt concluded in 1993 that delinquent behavior was a normal part of teenage life. While Dilulio argued that predatory teens should be locked in adult prisons for the safety of society, Moffitt and others argued that most teenagers outgrow delinquent behavior when they reach adulthood. They pointed to statistics indicating that criminal behavior peaks at age seventeen and then spirals downward. The arrest rates for twenty-five-year-olds are about half those for seventeen-year-olds.

Researchers were beginning to prove what parents and teachers knew instinctively—that teenagers are a different breed than adults. But there was little hard research to prove that adolescents think differently than adults even while they are acting like adults. What goes on inside the teenage brain was as much a mystery to psychologists, scientists, and researchers as it was to the average parent.

That acknowledgment of how little is known about what distinguishes the mentality of a teenager from that of an adult started Temple University developmental psychologist Laurence Steinberg thinking.

• • •

In the spring semester of 1995, Laurence Steinberg and Elizabeth Cauffman sat at a small round table in his cramped and narrow office on the fifth floor of Weiss Hall and debated the age at which a child should be tried as an adult. There was no consensus among the states. In Kansas and Vermont the minimum age was ten; in Missouri, twelve; in Illinois, thirteen; in Iowa, fourteen; in New Mexico, fifteen. In Florida there was no age limit.

Steinberg and Cauffman met on a day when he wasn't in the classroom, so the coat and tie were replaced by jeans and a long-sleeve button-down shirt. Steinberg was a short, somewhat portly man with a trim white beard who reminded some of Santa Claus and others of actor Richard Dreyfuss. He had begun working on a paper for the Mac Arthur Foundation, a Chicago-based philanthropic organization best known for its five-year "genius grants" to people who demonstrate exceptional creativity. The foundation also provided funding from its $5.24 billion endowment for research on social issues such as housing, education, and juvenile justice reform. Steinberg hoped to win Mac Arthur support to fund the research required to overturn the death penalty for juveniles. He was enlisting Cauffman, one of his brightest students, to help him do just that.

Cauffman was a twenty-two-year-old graduate student in search of a doctoral dissertation. In a sweater and jeans, with her backpack at her feet, she listened to Steinberg. He posed a simple question for which there was no simple answer: Where is the developmental line when a teenager possesses the ability to control impulses and think ahead? Cauffman knew it wasn't a question about the ability to know right from wrong—the legal standard of culpability. Her dog knows right from wrong: Good dog, bad dog. What Steinberg wanted to know was the age at which a teenager, knowing that something he or she is about to do is wrong, understands the consequences of those actions and does the right thing.

Not far from being a teenager herself, Cauffman argued for the older teenager: seventeen, eighteen, nineteen. Steinberg believed the opposite: fifteen or sixteen. But neither of them knew for sure. Their opinions were based on personal experience, anecdotal evidence, and what they saw on TV and read in the newspapers.

Before the hour was over, Cauffman had agreed to research the research, to see what scientific analysis existed on the physiological, mental, and emotional development of the modern-day adolescent. What she found was some evidence that adolescents under seventeen think differently than older teens, but much of the research in juvenile decision making was based on laboratory tests involving hypothetical situations. Little was known about how kids think when making real-world decisions that have serious consequences. Even less was known about how "psychosocial" influences—the presence of other teenagers, for example—affect the decisions made by adolescents.

In researching her dissertation, Cauffman went into the schools to test teenagers from sixth through twelfth grade to compare what she found among adults up to the age of forty-five. At first the data confounded her: sixth graders were as mature as forty-year-olds, but eighth graders were far less mature. When she went back and looked more closely, she discovered a pseudo-maturity among the youngest teens. At thirteen they were parroting their parents. By fifteen they were beginning to challenge and rebel, distancing themselves from their parents' sphere of influence. They were starting to think, rightly and wrongly, for themselves. This mistaken maturity in early adolescence contributed to the public—and political—view that children were growing up faster and earlier than ever before and committing the same crimes for the same reasons as adults.

A year after their first meeting in Steinberg's office, Cauffman and Steinberg published the findings of her dissertation as *Maturity of Judgment in Adolescence: Psychosocial Factors in Adolescent Decision Making*. In that paper they laid the foundation for the creation of the MacArthur Foundation Research Network on Adolescent Development and Juvenile Justice in 1997. The network, chaired by Steinberg, would assemble a dozen researchers and scholars on developmental psychology, social science, brain neurology, law, and criminal justice. Around a core of four experts—Steinberg; Thomas Grisso, a psychiatry professor at the University of Massachusetts medical school; Jeff Fagan, a professor of law and public health at Columbia University; and Ed Mulvey, director of the Law and Psychiatry Program at the University of Pittsburgh Medical School—the network began working to establish a scientific basis for the idea that adolescents engaged in crime think and act differently than adults.

Following the publication of *Maturity of Judgment in Adolescence* in 1996, the network released a series of papers on adolescent decision making, teenage culpability, and the competence of children to stand trial as adults.

In 2001, Steinberg and Cauffman published their findings on adolescents tried in adult court. In that paper they contended that the "blameworthiness" of teens differs from that of adults. Instead of the juvenile court system's assumption that all children are immature, and the adult system's presumption that they all are mature, adolescent development is a gradual, uneven process in which kids of the same age vary greatly in their ability to control impulses, think ahead, and understand the consequences of their actions. Instead of laws that draw "bright-line distinctions" between adolescence and adulthood, Steinberg and Cauffman argued, the legal system needed to acknowledge that not all seventeen-year-olds are the same.

Two years later, Steinberg, Cauffman, Grisso, and Elizabeth Scott (a professor at the University of Virginia law school), along with other researchers, released a study titled "Juveniles' Competence to Stand Trial as Adults" in which they challenged the idea that adolescents could participate in their own defense in adult court. Their study found that younger adolescents were more likely to be influenced by adult authority figures (including police officers and attorneys), were less able to assist in their own defense, and were unable to understand the long-term risks when confronted with basic legal decisions, such as plea bargains. In adult courts, they remain children with a child's perspective and deference to grown-ups. The study's findings struck at the heart of the trend of lowering the age for the prosecution of children as adults. Florida was one of several states that set no minimum age for charging juveniles—even elementary school children—as adults.

In December 2003, Steinberg and Scott published their rebuttal to the "adult time for adult crime" movement with their argument of "less guilty by reason of adolescence." They demonstrated an "immaturity gap" that showed the difference between intellectual maturity, which reaches adult levels at sixteen, and psychological maturity, which continues to develop well into the twenties. Juveniles, wrote Steinberg and Scott, were less culpable than adults for their actions because of shortsighted decision making, poor impulse control, and vulnerability to peer pressure.

In one study, given the choice, adolescents were far more likely than adults to take $100 now than $1,000 a year from now. In another study, juveniles demonstrated impatience and an inability to think ahead in a test that required them to solve a puzzle in as few moves as possible. When it came to peer pressure, a computer driving test showed that adolescents were more likely to drive recklessly while in the presence of other teens.

Moreover, Steinberg and Scott cited data from brain research to show the physical basis for these differences in thinking and behavior. The parts of the brain that regulate impulse control, planning, and thinking ahead are still developing at eighteen—precisely when the hormones in puberty increase the brain's desire for thrill seeking and risk taking, which also makes the adolescent more susceptible to peer influence. "Less guilty by reason of adolescence" doesn't mean teenagers are not responsible for their actions, Steinberg and Scott wrote, but it does mean they should not be judged, convicted, and punished the same as adults.

"The available evidence supports the conclusion that, like offenders who are mentally retarded and mentally ill, adolescents are less culpable than typical adults because of diminished decision-making capacity," they wrote. "The [U.S.] Supreme Court has repeatedly emphasized that the death penalty is acceptable punishment only for the most blameworthy killers."

• • •

Back in Pensacola, Martin Levin was using much the same argument in a lawsuit filed in 1991 by Sandra Faye Coker against Wal-Mart for selling to Patrick Bonifay and Eddie Fordham the bullets that killed her husband. In his brief, Levin cited some of the same evidence that juveniles are different from adults by University of Virginia clinical psychologist Dewey Cornell. "Dr. Cornell testified that efforts needed to be taken to keep guns and ammunition out of the hands of minors because minors are impulsive and irresponsible and do not have the maturity to deal with the peer pressure and emotions which arise by possessing a pistol," Levin wrote. "Minors gain a sense of power and intoxication by handling a gun and have a desire to prove themselves."

In his case against Wal-Mart, Levin argued that in the murder of Billy Wayne Coker, the only grown-up was the company that sold the bullets. "Wal-Mart was the adult here," Levin told an Escambia County Circuit Court jury. In assessing the blame for Coker's death, Levin argued that if Wal-Mart had not sold the bullets to underage teenagers, Coker would not have been killed. Under federal law, it is illegal to sell bullets for handguns to anyone under the age of twenty-one—and for good reason.

"Wal-Mart violated a federal law. What did they think was going to happen when they sold that ammunition? It was Saturday night at nine o'clock; two boys come in to buy pistol ammunition with no adult supervision," he argued. "What did Wal-Mart think was about to take place?" In all the moments of bad judgment on one fatal night, Levin argued, Wal-Mart was as negligent as Patrick, Eddie, and Cliff were culpable in Coker's death.

"What did it take to kill Billy Wayne Coker?" Levin asked. "It took three things. It took a gun, it took ammunition, it took someone willing to pull the trigger. [Kelly] Bland had the gun, Wal-Mart had the ammunition, and Bonifay had the finger."

The jury agreed. In a decision that surprised Levin as much as it did Wal-Mart, the jury placed more blame on the retail giant than on the boy who pulled the trigger, parsing out the liability for Coker's death as 35 percent Wal-Mart, 25 percent Patrick Bonifay, 25 percent Robin Archer, 8 percent Clifford Barth, and 7 percent Eddie Fordham.

The jury's reasoning was upheld by the First District Court of Appeal of Florida, which reaffirmed that Congress banned the sale of ammunition to minors because having guns and bullets in the hands of teenagers was likely to result in somebody getting shot. The law, the judges ruled, "was enacted to prevent the exact type of harm which occurred in this case." In 1997 the Florida Supreme Court upheld the ruling and ordered Wal-Mart to pay the Coker family $2.6 million.

Levin was assisted in his case against Wal-Mart by Patrick and Eddie, who agreed to provide video testimony that twenty-two-year-old

Wal-Mart store clerk Ken Powell never asked to see their identification or proof of age. Both teens believed that helping Sandra Coker win her case against Wal-Mart was one way for them to repay the widow for the loss of her husband's life.

The Wal-Mart lawsuit came as Patrick was beginning to reinvent himself.

Transformation 10

In 2001, ten years after Billy Wayne Coker's death, Patrick declared that the whole murder-for-hire story was a lie. Robin Archer had nothing to do with Coker's murder. There was never a suitcase of money. Archer wasn't seeking revenge against Wells for costing him his job at Trout Auto. Patrick was not a troubled boy manipulated by an older man to commit a murder; he was a desperate teenager looking for some fast money to instantly change his life. Archer told Patrick how he could rob Trout Auto, but he never told him to shoot the clerk in the head. Trout Auto was not a contract killing gone wrong. It was a robbery gone bad.

Patrick's own mother didn't believe him. Theresa was never sure what to believe when it came to Patrick. She was convinced that his new version of what happened inside Trout Auto was a legal strategy by Patrick's appeal attorney. Her son was running out of chances. In January 1994 the Florida Supreme Court upheld Patrick's murder conviction but declared that the jury improperly found that the murder was a heinous, atrocious, or cruel crime. The court ordered that

Patrick undergo resentencing by another jury. That jury, hearing the same evidence as the one that convicted him, came back with the same verdict: ten to two for the death penalty.

Theresa believed the recanting was Patrick's last attempt to escape death row by reducing his felony murder conviction to second-degree murder or manslaughter. If he had not told detective Tom O'Neal that an older adult, Archer, had bribed and then coerced him into killing the clerk, he'd be out of prison by now.

On February 26, 2001, in the same Pensacola courthouse where ten years earlier he had been convicted and sentenced to death, Patrick stood before Circuit Court Judge Michael Jones with his new attorney, Gregory Farrar. The first thing Jones asked Patrick was if he knew that Farrar was opposed to what he was about to do.

"Absolutely," Patrick replied.

"Alright," Jones said. "What is it that you would like to communicate?"

"This month, your honor, has been ten years of this going on. And the truth is, your honor, I'm tired. And there was no contract, there was no suitcase full of money, there was no hit," Patrick said. "There was a robbery. And I'm going to have to stand before the law on Judgment Day and answer for one man's blood on my hands. I ain't going to answer for two. There was no contract. There was no hit. That's just something I made up trying to get away from getting into trouble, putting it on somebody else."

Archer's attorney quickly filed an appeal to overturn Patrick's conviction based on his new confession. The teenager whose testimony was essential to Archer's conviction was admitting he made it all up and had sent an innocent man to death row.

A year later, Judge Jones conducted a post-conviction hearing on whether Patrick's recantation justified overturning Archer's conviction. If Jones accepted Patrick's new story, it could be grounds for overturning Archer's conviction and would remove two of the elements that made Coker's murder a capital offense punishable by death: premeditation and murder for money.

To Patrick, his recantation was his public declaration that he was no longer the boy he once was. He was, in fact, no longer Patrick Bonifay. He was Nabiyl Taqqi Ya'quib Musaaleh, a devout Muslim.

Theresa had doubts about her son's conversion to Islam. He was a white boy in a predominantly black prison system looking for protection. The Muslims on death row were just a different kind of gang. Patrick the disciple of Islam was another of his fantasy lives.

Patrick insisted that his personal and religious transformation was genuine, part of a process that began with the death of his grandfather from a heart attack in November 1991. The death of James Scarbrough was a shock. Patrick felt, for the first time on death row, utterly alone. Scarbrough was the last person on earth who really cared about him, the only one who seemed to understand the wild child inside him. They had spoken only once since Patrick's arrest. Patrick was in the Escambia County Jail when his grandfather called. The last words Patrick heard him say were "I pray they will give you another chance."

From his cell, Patrick began to question himself, his foreseeable death, the reason for his existence, the purpose of whatever life he had left. The loss of his grandfather and the prospect of losing his own life sent Patrick in search of explanations. Death row could make him insane, or make him insightful.

Patrick had always been an argumentative kid, and plenty of people on death row were willing to debate him on the subjects of life, death, and God. Religion became his sanctuary, a place that offered hope, forgiveness, and redemption; it provided answers. Patrick burrowed into the Bible, explored Buddhism and Hinduism, and read the Koran. He noticed that the Muslims on death row had a sense of serenity that other inmates lacked. When he debated religion with them on the exercise yard, Islam made more sense to him than the Christianity he espoused. In the ritual of daily prayer and meditation, the wisdom of the Koran, and the calm self-assurance of other Muslim prisoners, Patrick felt he had found the rain to extinguish the rage inside his soul. His religious conversion came in small increments of reading and thinking about Islam on his cell bunk before he reached the conclusion that Islam was the path he should follow to the end of his life. It gave him a framework for self-discipline and soul-searching. He asked himself, *How can I be at odds with a belief that takes a man who is the scourge of society and turns him into an intelligent, composed, disciplined, self-respecting man?*

Islam, the unfamiliar religion Patrick discovered in prison, became his obsession. When he spoke to his mother, Islam was all he wanted to talk about. In every way that death row was confining, stressful, monotonous, sensory-deprived, and soul-destroying, Islam was liberating, calming, stimulating, and life-affirming. Outside his cell, he wore chains at all times. Within his mind, he was unchained by religion.

Six years into his death sentence, Patrick converted to Islam. His Muslim name—Nabiyl Taqqi Ya'quib Musaaleh—meant "Noble, God-fearing Supplanter; One Who Makes Peace." Islam allowed him to change not only his religion but also his identity. He wasn't the emotionally troubled delinquent adrift and alone on the streets of Pensacola or the would-be warrior in a Marine's uniform. He wasn't the kid nobody could control and nobody wanted. He was Nabiyl, disciple of Shaykh Togun Bayrak al-Jerrahi, a boy no longer but a twenty-four-year-old man who understood himself through his understanding of Allah. On his left arm, he obliterated the handmade tattoo of the heart with his old girlfriend's name, Rae, in the middle by covering it with a prison tattoo of a green crescent, the Koran, and crossed Chechen daggers. Above the design he etched the words "God is enough for us" in Arabic.

Patrick Bonifay as Nabiyl Musaaleh believed himself to be a new man, shedding the skin of his past. Patrick was immature; Nabiyl was responsible. Patrick was impulsive; Nabiyl was disciplined. Patrick was demanding; Nabiyl was accepting. Patrick was vengeful; Nabiyl was forgiving. Patrick was sorry; Nabiyl was remorseful.

The eleven-year-old boy who said his three wishes were to have $10 million, live with his mother, and fish with his stepfather was now a devout Muslim whose two wishes were to visit Mecca and to shed the tears of his ignorance at the grave of Billy Wayne Coker.

Nabiyl could not bring back to life the man Patrick killed, but he could still save the life of Robin Lee Archer. Patrick's testimony had helped to convict Archer. Nabiyl would try to convince the courts that Patrick had lied.

• • •

As a devout Muslim, Patrick believed it was his obligation to speak the truth to free Archer from death row, but the court was unconvinced.

Too many lies for too many years. "Based on the Court's experience, common sense, and personal observations of Patrick Bonifay, the Court is satisfied that this new testimony is false," Judge Jones wrote. "After listening to Mr. Bonifay, observing his demeanor, and analyzing his testimony, the Court does not believe his recantation."

The judge's decision would later be upheld by the Florida Supreme Court.

The courts' rejection of his recantation came as no surprise to Patrick. The judges and lawyers believe what they want to believe, Patrick told himself. A prosecutor can present him as both a reliable witness and a bald-faced liar. An unbelievable story about a suitcase full of money can be accepted as fact, but the religious conversion of a condemned man is suspect and untrue. A scared seventeen-year-old boy trying to save his own life is more believable than a grown man who has spent a decade on death row.

I did what I could, Patrick told himself. I'm still in prison, but I freed myself by telling the truth. I'm not helping the state kill Robin Archer.

. . .

Patrick didn't get a chance to tell Archer of his remorse in person. Despite their years together on the same death row, awaiting the same fate, the two never met or spoke to each other again. Nor did Patrick ever meet or speak with the two other men who were seventeen when they were sentenced to die. Cleo Douglas LeCroy had been on death row the longest, sentenced in 1986. Nathaniel Ramirez received the death penalty in 1996 for the rape and murder of a seventy-one-year-old woman in New Port Richey. There were twenty-nine more teenagers just like them awaiting execution in Texas.

Religious conversion and a different story couldn't save Patrick from Florida's electric chair, but halfway across the country the case of another seventeen-year-old boy on Missouri's death row had begun an incremental crawl toward the U.S. Supreme Court. A seismic shift was under way in how the United States viewed youthful killers.

Christopher Simmons was a teenager very much like Patrick Bonifay.

Hope 11

The worst room in the house for fifteen-year-old Christopher Simmons was the bathroom. In the mirror, his face was ablaze with pimples. His stepfather, the man he called Dad, had his own way of treating teenage acne.

Much like Patrick Bonifay, Christopher was the product of a brief and stormy marriage. Married five years, Dennis and Cheryl Simmons were separated when Christopher was born on April 26, 1976. Cheryl accused Dennis of being an alcoholic, a compulsive gambler, and a womanizer. Dennis claimed Cheryl was an unfaithful wife who left him for Bob Hayes while still pregnant with Chris.

Hayes was no better. He was a heavy-drinking, hard-partying truck driver with a quick temper that he took out on Christopher. On the street where they lived in Fenton, Missouri, a small suburb outside St. Louis, neighbors could see, and hear, Hayes beating the boy with a belt, dragging him around by the ear, slapping him on the head, and verbally berating him.

Hayes became obsessed with Christopher's acne. If he walked into the bathroom when Christopher stepped from the shower,

Hayes attacked his son's acne like it was a disease curable by force. He scrubbed Christopher's face with gritty Lava soap. He pinched the pimples on the boy's face and neck. He used needles on the pustules.

If Christopher resisted, Hayes shoved him against the wall or pinned him on the floor. If the boy cried or whimpered, Hayes taunted him for being weak, a sissy, a girl trapped inside a boy's body. On the floor, Christopher seethed with hatred and fear. He hid those feelings from Hayes, learning never to look him in the eyes. Growing up, Christopher kept his gaze on the ground.

On the floor of the bathroom, Christopher was directly above the basement of the three-bedroom, one-bath home at the end of Oak Drive. The basement was his sanctuary, and his exile. Banished to the basement when his two younger brothers were born, Christopher had the place to himself. It was a mouse-infested, dank, musty-smelling subterranean room that leaked a stream of water that ran crossways through the carpet when it rained hard. His bed was a fold-out couch. He had his own TV and an eight-track player built into the wall where he listened to his parents' Black Sabbath tapes.

A couple of broken-down arcade games stood in a corner from the days when his mother and father ran a little grocery store down the street. Bob and Cheryl Hayes never had much money. While Bob was driving a truck, Cheryl worked as a dental assistant. They owned the house, but they had to mortgage it a couple of times, and at least once they filed for bankruptcy. But they had enough money to afford a couple of VCRs and shelves of movies, many of them duped. The top shelf held Hayes's porn collection.

In a back room of the basement was a table with a train set where, as a child, Christopher tried to share an interest with his stepfather. Most of the time he just ended up annoying Hayes, as often happened during these attempts at bonding. Once, when Christopher was a toddler, Hayes took him fishing, got drunk, and tied him to a tree for hours so he wouldn't wander off.

In the basement was a wet bar with bottles of liquor that Christopher pilfered and a revolving lamp that said "The Bar Is Open." He started drinking young. When Christopher was a little kid, Hayes used to bring him along to the bars and force him to get drunk for the amusement of his buddies.

On the street where Christopher grew up, there was a woods to play in until it was replaced by a trailer park. There were lots of kids to play with, and some of them came from the trailer park. Christopher would invite a couple of them over, and they'd spend their time in the basement listening to Nirvana, Steve Miller, and Metallica while smoking cigarettes, drinking, and getting high on pot.

By age thirteen, Christopher was drinking and using drugs. The booze and pot were one form of escape; the other was to run away. The first time he ran away, in 1994, he was gone for two weeks, crashing at the home of a friend. For the next two years, Christopher would seek sanctuary with his friend's family several times a week, sometimes sleeping in a shed in the backyard.

When Christopher ran away, his mother seldom went looking for him. His absence provided a reprieve from the constant conflict between her husband and her son. She wouldn't go after him, but if she saw him on the street she would coax him into coming back home, and it would all start over again.

Before he began smoking pot, drinking, and running away, Christopher was an average student. By the time he was seventeen and a junior at Fox High School, he had fifty-two absences, a GPA of .846, and a ranking of 520th in his class of 533 students.

Eventually, Christopher started hanging out at the trailer of Brian Moomey. Moomey was much like Robin Archer—a twenty-nine-year-old ex-con who encouraged teenagers to commit crimes for him. In return, Moomey provided the juveniles with a parent-free place where they could drink, use drugs, and get homemade tattoos. Moomey's trailer became a party pad for teenagers such as Christopher and a fifteen-year-old named Charlie Benjamin. Charlie and Christopher knew each other well. They played basketball, raced bikes through the neighborhood, and broke into homes together.

Before 2 A.M. on September 9, 1993, Christopher, Charlie, and sixteen-year-old John Tessner left Moomey's trailer to burglarize a home. Tessner backed out before they reached the house of Shirley Ann Cook. Christopher found a back window of the home cracked open, reached inside, and unlocked a back door.

Shirley Cook awoke when Christopher turned on a hallway light. She sat up in her bed.

"Who's there?" she said.

When Christopher walked into the bedroom, they recognized each other from a previous traffic accident. Fearing she would identify him, Christopher wrapped duct tape around her eyes and mouth and bound her arms behind her back. Charlie and Christopher led Cook outside and into her 1988 Ford Aerostar minivan. They drove sixteen miles to Castlewood State Park, where they tied a towel around her head, marched her out onto a railroad trestle, and bound her hands and feet with a strap from her purse, the belt from her robe, and some electrical wire they found on the trestle. Christopher pushed her off the bridge, forty feet above the Meramec River. Alive as she fell, Cook drowned in the water.

The next day, Christopher was sitting in a counselor's office at Fox High School when five police officers in two patrol cars pulled up in front of the school. Moomey had told them that Christopher had bragged about the murder, saying he killed some woman because the bitch saw his face. Christopher could see the police coming down the hall, heading toward his classroom. His instinct, as always, was to run. As he stood up, the school's assistant principal blocked the door. Christopher sat back down and waited for the police to arrest him. They led him from the school in handcuffs.

Arrested for murder, Christopher was interrogated by police and signed a confession without his parents present or notified. Police took him back to Cook's house and videotaped him reenacting the crime.

Because of his age, Charlie Benjamin was sentenced to life without parole. Christopher, because of his, was sentenced to die in the electric chair.

His execution scheduled for 12:01 A.M. on May 1, 2002, Christopher Simmons became the surrogate for Patrick Bonifay and seventy other juvenile inmates on death row when the U.S. Supreme Court heard arguments in *Roper v. Simmons* in 2004. The justices were asked to determine whether the death penalty should apply to juveniles. In 1989 the Court had ruled that sixteen- and seventeen-year-olds were old enough to be executed. Since then, however, pressure had been mounting to move the bar closer to the standard observed by the rest of the world. Among the world's nations, the United States stood alone in the execution of juveniles, left behind in recent years by Iran, Pakistan, China, Saudi Arabia, Yemen, Nigeria, and the Republic of Congo. Canada, England, France, Germany, Italy, and Japan all set twenty-one as the benchmark for capital punishment. Christopher Simmons moved beyond being a stand-in for death-row teens and became an international symbol of the United States' barbaric notion of justice.

Former President Jimmy Carter, former Soviet President Mikhail Gorbachev, Archbishop Desmond Tutu of South Africa, Polish labor leader Lech Walesa, and the Dalai Lama joined a group of Nobel laureates who argued that the United States had no moral authority to criticize other countries for human rights violations as long as it executed juveniles.

In advance of the oral arguments before the Supreme Court on October 13, 2004, a joint brief filed by the American Medical Association, the American Psychiatric Association, the American Society for Adolescent Psychiatry, the American Academy of Child and Adolescent Psychiatry, the American Academy of Psychiatry and the Law, and the National Association of Social Workers presented the latest scientific evidence that distinguished the brains of juveniles from those of mature adults.

"The adolescent's mind works differently from ours. Parents know it. This Court has said it. Legislatures have presumed it for decades or more. And now, new scientific evidence sheds light on the differences," their argument began. "Cutting-edge brain imaging technology reveals that regions of the adolescent brain do not reach a fully mature state until after the age of 18. These regions are precisely those associated with impulse control, regulation of emotions, risk assessment, and moral reasoning. Critical developmental changes in these regions occur only after late adolescence."

Together, the medical, psychological, and juvenile justice advocates represented before the Supreme Court a growing movement against use of the death penalty for teenagers. At the center of their argument was the work of Laurence Steinberg and the MacArthur Foundation Research Network.

Developmental neuroscience confirmed what parents and teachers have known forever: Teenagers do not think the same way adults do. Brain-imaging technology and performance tests that compared teenagers to adults found that the brain's frontal lobe, which controls the mind's "executive functions," is still developing in adolescence. That part of the brain—the dorsal lateral prefrontal cortex—affects the ability to control impulses, plan ahead, and weigh the risks and consequences of an action.

At the same time, the adolescent limbic system is bristling with receptors for dopamine, the pleasure transmitter, and oxytocin, a hormone important for social bonding. Together, they provide the groundwork for reckless, thrill-seeking behavior, especially among a group of peers. This helped explain why crimes committed by teens were more often done in groups, while adult criminals were more likely to act alone.

The American Psychological Association (APA) joined the case with an amicus brief of its own. APA attorney Nathalie Gilfoyle, in her preparation of the brief, worked closely with Steinberg and Thomas Grisso, going over the research that delved deeply into the brains, thinking, and behavior of teenagers. In the brief, her job was to translate the science into a legal argument that made sense to the nine Supreme Court justices. For it to make sense to them, it had to make sense to her.

Gilfoyle's aha moment came during a lecture on the methods used to determine if someone is a psychopath. The assessment checklist for a psychopath—need for stimulation, impulsiveness, irresponsibility, lack of empathy, failure to accept responsibility, and a grandiose sense of self-worth—sounded strikingly familiar to Gilfoyle, the mother of two teenage boys. The characteristics of the teen and the psychopath were so close, in fact, that the test can't be used on people under the age of eighteen. This revelation confirmed for Gilfoyle the argument she would make for Christopher Simmons: Psychopathic behavior in an adult is set in stone, but the same behavior in a teenager is a common but transitory stage of development that can't be used to predict who that person will become. The proof of the hypothesis was inside her own life, Gilfoyle thought: *I was such a bad teenager.*

In the brief supporting the idea that teenagers should not be eligible for the death penalty, Gilfoyle argued that even the worst juvenile offenders—those labeled psychopaths or sociopaths—may be misdiagnosed. Because the adolescent brain is a "moving target," any attempt to assess a teen's personality and future dangerousness—two important factors in applying the death penalty—is prone to error. Moreover, while psychopathic traits in an adult are an accurate predictor of future behavior, those same characteristics in a teenager are likely to diminish as the adolescent matures.

"Assessments of such severe antisocial behaviors during adolescence have yet to be shown to remain stable as individuals grow into adulthood," Gilfoyle's brief argued. "Consequently, attempts to predict at capital sentencing an adolescent offender's character formation and dangerousness in adulthood are inherently prone to error and create an obvious risk of wrongful execution."

. . .

From his cell on death row, thirty-year-old Patrick Bonifay read about what his brain looked like at seventeen. Barred from accessing the Internet, he devoured every piece of paper he could read on *Roper v. Simmons*. He bored into the details of the arguments like baseball fans read the box scores. From records provided by opponents of the death penalty, Patrick studied the briefs filed by both sides and the transcripts of the debate that took place in the marbled courtroom of the nine Supreme Court justices.

In 2005, Patrick was thirteen years into his life on death row. During those years, thirty-one men and one woman were executed in Florida. On Starke's death row, just a short distance from the execution chamber, Patrick had lived through the death of Nollie Lee Martin on May 12, 1992, of Edward Kennedy on July 21, 1992, of Robert Henderson on April 21, 1992, and of Larry Johnson on May 8, 1993.

After the head of Pedro Medina—a Muslim inmate—caught fire during his execution in 1997, the state instituted lethal injection in 2000 as an alternative to the electric chair. Death-row inmates were allowed to choose how they would die: electrocution or lethal injection.

In his study of the court transcripts and amicus briefs and his correspondence with death-penalty opponents outside the prison, Patrick became convinced that neither lethal injection nor electrocution was in his future. He began discussing with corrections officials the prisons to which he would like to be transferred. His list included facilities where he could complete his high school education, since death row, the holding pen for terminal prisoners, did not offer GED classes. Prison officials were blunt: it would be a waste of public money to educate men whom the state was going to execute.

On March 1, 2005, the U.S. Supreme Court released its ruling. By a vote of five to four, the Court ruled that the United States should join the rest of the world in prohibiting the death penalty for juveniles under the age of eighteen. Writing for the majority, Justice Anthony Kennedy cited three major differences between adolescents and adults that precluded classifying adolescents as society's worst offenders and subject to the ultimate penalty: first was the lack of maturity and sense of responsibility among teenagers; second was their vulnerability and susceptibility to negative influences and peer pressure; and third was the transitory personality of juveniles, whose sense of self is still forming.

Acting as the supreme parent of the nation's legal system, the majority of the Court recognized what parents—and the rest of the world—had long ago acknowledged: Teenagers are out of their minds. They act mature and sophisticated one minute and regress into infantile behavior the next. They have the capacity to think rationally and the intellect to solve complex problems, but they act on impulses and urges. They occupy the murky, maddening otherworld between the child and the adult—a part of both, belonging to neither. They are not yet fully formed persons.

"The reality that juveniles still struggle to define their identity means it is less supportable to conclude that even a heinous crime committed by a juvenile is evidence of irretrievably depraved character," Kennedy wrote on behalf of the majority, along with Stephen Breyer, David Souter, Ruth Bader Ginsburg, and John Paul Stevens. "From a moral standpoint it would be misguided to equate the failings of a minor with those of an adult, for a greater possibility exists that a minor's character deficiencies will be reformed." Echoing Steinberg's catchphrase—"less guilty by reason of adolescence"—Kennedy wrote that neither retribution nor deterrence could justify imposing the death penalty for juvenile killers.

"Whether viewed as an attempt to express the community's moral outrage or as an attempt to right the balance for the wrong to the victim, the base for retribution is not as strong with a minor as with an adult. Retribution is not proportional if the law's most severe penalty is imposed on one whose culpability or blameworthiness is diminished, to a substantial degree, by reason of youth and immaturity," Kennedy wrote. "As for deterrence, it is unclear whether the death penalty has a significant or even measurable deterrent effect on juveniles. . . . [T]he same characteristics that render juveniles less culpable than adults suggest as well that juveniles will be less susceptible to deterrence. . . . [T]he likelihood that the teenage offender has made the kind of cost-benefit analysis that attaches any weight to the possibility of execution is so remote as to be virtually nonexistent."

Kennedy didn't excuse or minimize the fact that teenagers are capable of violent, brutal crimes that inflict tremendous suffering on the victim and the victim's family. But he reiterated the argument that a teen who commits murder is not the same as an adult who commits murder, because the juvenile killer is, in fact, still maturing. A juvenile should still be punished for committing a murder, but the punishment should be different from that for a fully formed adult: "When a juvenile offender commits a heinous crime, the State can exact forfeiture of some of the most basic liberties, but the State cannot extinguish his life and his potential to attain a mature understanding of his own humanity."

In the majority's opinion, the Court seemed swayed by the evolving standards of decency represented by the dwindling number of states that execute juveniles and the "stark reality" that the United States stood alone in executing teenagers. The Court further noted that the death penalty for juveniles violated several international treaties, including the Geneva Accords and the United Nations Convention on the Rights of the Child.

In essence, the U.S. Supreme Court bent to international peer pressure: "It is proper that we acknowledge the overwhelming weight of international opinion against the juvenile death penalty, resting in large part on the understanding that the instability and emotional imbalance of young people may often be a factor in the crime," Kennedy concluded for the majority.

•   •   •

Official notice from the Florida Supreme Court of his release from death row came as Patrick was reading the transcripts of Anthony Kennedy and Antonin Scalia arguing both sides of *Roper v. Simmons*. He unfolded the paper, dated July 25, 2005, looked at it, and said to himself, "I'm out of here."

Patrick felt no sense of relief or delight with the ruling. His mind had left death row long before his body would. He wasn't a boy anymore, but he felt like he was back inside that van on his way to Lake Butler fourteen years earlier, wondering what was ahead of him, where he would end up, what it would be like to be among a general population of prisoners.

Am I in a dorm full of Crips? Am I in a dorm full of Aryans? Am I in a dorm full of skinheads? I might be locked in a room with another man who could be a bug, who may be a rapist. Am I going to have to beat this dude half to death in the middle of the night?

When the prison bus came to take him away from the death row at Raiford, Patrick, still in shackles and chains, was the only one to get aboard. He rode alone until the bus stopped at Starke, picked up more prisoners, and took everyone to Columbia Correctional Institution, where he was transferred to a bus that would take him to his new prison, Jackson Correctional Institution, near the Florida-Alabama border. Before his bus left, two prisoners—one black, the other Hispanic—got into a bloody fight. Guards pulled the bleeding Cuban off the bus and left the black inmate in his seat. *Damn!* Patrick thought, *it's starting already*.

At Jackson he was led to H-dorm and a two-man cell he would share with an inmate from Miami who called himself Thin Man. Patrick felt like a man in shock—after all those years of isolation, deprivation, and chains, he was now in this sea of men and movement and noise and chaos. His senses were on high alert, his emotions a cocktail of fear and elation. The sight of a squirrel surprised him. A simple oak tree looked majestic. He took off his shoes to walk in the grass and remembered what it had felt like to run barefoot as a kid in Pensacola. He lay down on the grass and rolled around, laughing and smiling. The sky, confined and constricted in the death-row yard, was wide open and wonderful here. In the predawn morning, walking to breakfast, he was astounded by the moon and the stars.

But in the exercise yard, the halls, and the dorms and cafeteria, Patrick viewed every guard as a potential threat, every prisoner a potential enemy. For the first time in fourteen years in prison, he felt vulnerable and scared. He wasn't on death row, where everyone was a murderer; at Jackson he was tossed in with rapists, punks, gang members, thugs, molesters, robbers, and thieves. The guards might be sadists, bitter losers, or bullies with batons. Every move he made was preceded by a mental calculus: *I have to go from here to there. The people here and there are liable to be dangerous.*

In his first months at Jackson, Patrick felt he had been released into a madhouse. Inmates stabbing each other half to death in the yard, getting their heads busted in the dormitory. Death row was shackles and chains; Jackson was totally off the chain.

Thin Man helped him adjust. Both of them had been at Starke, and they knew some of the same inmates. If Patrick got jumpy when other prisoners stared at him, Thin Man would calm him down: "Nabiyl! People are staring at you 'cause you off death row, you a white Muslim, you walking around barefoot, and you intimidate some of them and they trying to figure you out," he said.

Mind your own business—the rule at Jackson was the same as it was at Starke and Raiford. Free from the constriction and isolation of death row, Patrick formed his own walls within the prison. He kept to himself and avoided other prisoners. He made friends cautiously, mostly with other Muslims. He ignored the guards who made fun of his kufi or challenged his faith: A Muslim white guy, huh?

If Islam soothed the torture in his soul, martial arts released the tension within his body. Other prisoners played basketball; Patrick practiced kicks and karate chops. He had always thought of himself as an exceptional fighter, and now he was becoming a well-trained martial artist. He bragged that he could throw a thousand punches in under seven minutes. Some prisoners believed him. He began training younger guys, the ones with level heads, in martial arts. He started thinking of himself as a prison personal trainer and imagining that the best of the ones he worked with might become light-heavyweight champions of the world when they got out.

For Patrick, there was no getting out. *No getting out*. When the thought surfaced, he buried it behind the fantasies that had always been his refuge when he couldn't escape. The boy who dreamed of marrying the girl, joining the Marines, and being stationed in Japan became the man who dreamed of being released from prison on a felony military waiver to fight in Afghanistan. He could see the headline: "Former Death Row Inmate Earns Silver Star in Afghanistan." The kid from the dysfunctional family imagined himself outside the prison walls as the patriarch of his clan, providing strength and guidance to another generation of Bonifays. The boy who liked to fight saw himself as an adult opening a mixed martial-arts gym to train Ultimate Fighters. A poor boy who once talked of a briefcase full of half a million dollars envisioned himself as a man of wealth living on an estate with Arabian horses. A guy who never had a driver's license listed the Jaguar as his favorite car, the Italian-made Ducati as his favorite motorcycle. If he had a horse, it would be a majestic Andalusian. If he had a dog, it would be the exotic Presa Canario. Confined to a prison dorm, he made a list of five things to do before he died: go to the Kentucky Derby; visit Ireland and Spain, the lands of his ancestors; watch the British Isle of Man motorcycle race; meet his spiritual teacher; and make a pilgrimage to Mecca and Medina. He envisioned making enough money from his ideas for books, the Muslim board game he concocted, and the inventions he envisioned to hire that Tallahassee lawyer who guaranteed his freedom for twenty thousand dollars.

Religion bestowed faith; fantasy conveyed hope. Imagining the impossible made the inevitable less real and relieved the dull, unchanging ritual of prison life—the head counts, the meals at five, eleven, and four, lights out at ten. Imagination kept Patrick afloat, lifted him above the chain-link fences, the coils of razor wire, and the guard towers that loomed like unblinking eyes. On death row he had learned how to save his sanity by never allowing his mind to become imprisoned. But one thought never completely disappeared: the awful understanding that in being spared the death penalty he was now condemned to life. *I'll die in prison.*

Life in prison with no chance of parole presented a different kind of cruelty. To Patrick, being condemned to death meant that society wanted revenge for what he had done: kill the monster. Being condemned to life meant that society had decided he was beyond redemption, that he could never be rehabilitated, that he was the same person at thirty-five that he was at seventeen, and that he would remain unchanged at fifty and sixty and seventy.

In many ways, Patrick the middle-aged man was still Patrick the teenage boy. Prison doesn't allow a juvenile to move through the stages and responsibilities of life that produce a mature adult. All the things that Patrick, Eddie, and Cliff missed out on in prison—graduating from high school, getting a job, losing a job, finding another, going to college, renting an apartment, paying the utility bill, getting married, having children, watching them grow up—are the transformative rites of passage into adulthood. Patrick regarded himself as a new man with a new name and new religion, but in many respects he remained unchanged, a man in age only preserved in prison as a child.

In his loneliest hours, Patrick longed for the certainty of death row. In his darkest days came the dreadful thought, *I'd be better off dead.*

Epilogue

P. Michael Patterson

On July 24, 1991, a week after the trials of Patrick Bonifay and Robin Archer, President George H. W. Bush appointed Judge Lacey Collier to the U.S. Federal Court. Two years later, Mike Patterson followed Collier to the federal courts, appointed by President Bill Clinton to become U.S. Attorney for the Northern District of Florida. Patterson remained a federal attorney until the purge by President George W. Bush's Attorney General Alberto Gonzales in 2001. He returned to Pensacola to join a law firm that specializes in personal injury, medical malpractice, and complex civil litigation.

Robin Lee Archer

Despite Patrick Bonifay's recantation, Robin Lee Archer remains on Florida's death row, awaiting execution.

Three years after entering prison, Eddie Fordham stopped wearing a watch. The routine of prison life became his timepiece: Headcounts at 7 A.M., 11:30 A.M., 4 P.M., 6:15 P.M., and 10 P.M. He has no use for a calendar. Every day in prison is a reenactment of the day before. The holidays that people outside prison anticipate and celebrate go by as another day inside Polk Correctional Institution in the middle of rural central Florida.

On Father's Day, he calls his dad, Larry Fordham Sr., who has moved with Diana to Slidell, Louisiana. He waits his turn on the second floor of his prison dorm to use the pay phone. Calls are limited to fifteen minutes, unless there's no one waiting. On this Father's Day, Eddie has to keep the conversation short. Larry answers the kitchen phone.

"Hey, happy Father's Day," Eddie says. "I thought I'd call you all earlier before you go to church."

"I got your card," Larry says. "It was very nice. I got it sitting on my chest of drawers."

"Did you see the golfer on the front?" Eddie asks.

"Yeah, but it didn't look like me."

"You don't think so?"

"Well, maybe back in the day," his father replies. "When I was slender."

"The chaplain passed out those cards, and most of the cards that I saw were, you know, kind of cheesy and everything," Eddie says. "And I just kind of lucked up and got that one, and I thought man, that's awesome because that's my dad's sport. He likes to play golf."

Before the conversation ends, Larry tells his son about the new neighbors they met, a couple from Stuart, Florida, and how they took them out on their pontoon boat the other day, through the canals around the neighborhood, just relaxing and enjoying each other's company. Eddie thanks his father for the new pair of tennis shoes and asks that he give Mom a hug and a kiss for him.

After nearly twenty years of dedicating themselves to winning Eddie's release, the Fordhams moved on. They made a new life for themselves in Louisiana, far away from Pensacola and their son's prison.

But for ten years after Eddie's conviction, Larry and Diana were their son's surrogates to the outside world of kids just like him—boys and girls who made poor choices of friends and poor decisions under the influence of others. From that first letter printed in the *Pensacola News Journal* the day after his conviction, Eddie wrote frequently to his hometown newspaper, preaching a cautionary tale of "false friends." His mantra—"Choose Your Friends Wisely"—became the slogan for Youth Awareness, Inc., a nonprofit organization his parents started in 1996 for teenagers on the edge of delinquency.

Youth Awareness became Eddie's cause, the purpose he fashioned out of his punishment, and it became his parents' passion and livelihood. Larry gave up his insurance business. Diana gave up her pursuit of social climbing. They obtained state and federal juvenile justice grants to conduct weeklong classes for teenagers, using Eddie's life and jail tours to redirect children from the bad influences of their peers.

For a while everything went well, but eventually the funding disappeared, and when the money vanished, Youth Awareness went into hiatus as Larry and Diana moved to Louisiana in 2008 to work for the government as post-Katrina flood-insurance specialists.

As Eddie approaches middle age, his face has filled out but is still boyish. His auburn hair, neatly cut, is often hidden beneath a broad-brimmed straw hat he wears outside to shield his skin from the sun. On his chest are small scars, like cat scratches, where doctors have removed spots of melanoma. He is beginning to experience the ills of middle age, including weight gain and high cholesterol. He started running for exercise. His requests for a diet with less starch have been largely ignored.

For the past several years, Eddie has worked as a computer programmer for PRIDE, a prison-based program that provides the state with free computer services. In his spare time he studies the latest computer programming languages, preparing himself for what comes next after his sentence is up. Eddie will be forty-four years old when he is eligible for parole in 2016.

In 1998, Florida Governor Jeb Bush denied Eddie's request for clemency. Just three years earlier, Sandra Faye Coker and Diana

Fordham had become friends for at least one day. A friend of Sandra's had arranged for the two women to meet, and when that friend died in March 1995, Sandra called Diana, and Diana offered her a ride to the funeral.

Their relationship didn't end there. Sandra's children had never been on the Pensacola Naval Air Station, and Diana, whose father had spent thirty-nine years on the base, offered to give them a tour, taking them to visit the grave of Geronimo's wife, the old lighthouse, the hangar of the Blue Angels, the *Lexington* aircraft carrier. Afterwards, they ate together at Barnhill's Restaurant.

On the way to the restaurant, Diana drove over a bridge and felt Sandra tense up, her hands latching onto anything she could grab as if she were in a roller coaster on its ascent.

"Sandra," Diana said. "It's just a short bridge."

"But you don't know me," Sandra replied. "I'm scared to go across bridges."

The day ended back at the Fordham house in Warrington with Michelle and Christopher swimming in the pool where Eddie used to play.

When Governor Jeb Bush denied Eddie's clemency, Sandra Coker's words came back to haunt Diana Fordham: "But you don't know me." In a letter to Bush, Sandra asked that Eddie be denied an early release, convinced that he was a willing participant in her husband's murder.

With no possibility of their son's release until 2016, Larry and Diana flew to Orlando to visit their son at the Polk Correctional Institution on February 6, 2009. It was the first time they had seen him since May 2008. The thirty-mile drive from Orlando to Polk City took longer than they expected, and when they arrived at 9:45 A.M. all the covered, concrete picnic tables in the prison courtyard were filled.

His mother cried as they embraced. His father, who had always been clean-shaven, looked distinguished in his new goatee. Diana wore a plastic anti-abortion bracelet on her wrist that said "All Life Is Precious." Both Larry and Diana had on Mickey Mouse watches.

While Eddie talked to his parents, a girl from his high school sneaked up from behind and wrapped her arms around him. Eddie hadn't seen Brandy Bartol since his conviction, and she hadn't visited him since she moved to Winter Park, forty-eight miles away from the prison.

Each had changed. They weren't kids in high school anymore but two middle-aged adults. Brandy wore a silver necklace with a pendant in the shape of a hinged box. Inside the box was a pinch of her father's cremated ashes. On her left hand was a long scar that wasn't there in high school. She had been in a car accident, Brandy told Eddie as he held her hand in his palm and traced the length of the scar with his finger.

They didn't talk about it that day, but each remembered the moment when their paths diverged as teenagers. Eddie was leaving a party at Bernadette Hefferton's house while her parents were away. Brandy was just arriving. They had never been girlfriend-boyfriend, but Brandy liked Eddie enough to confront him with her fears. She didn't like the Brown Boyz he was hanging out with. He had quit the high school swim team and started smoking. This wasn't the Eddie she had a crush on, the cute, sweet boy who she wished had the nerve to kiss her.

"Listen, you need to stop hanging around with these guys," she told him. "I don't know why you're doing this, but you're going to get into big trouble."

"Brandy, I'm a good guy," Eddie replied. "Nothing is going to happen to me. Everything is fine."

He didn't realize it then, but true friendship was staring him in the face outside Bernadette Hefferton's house.

As Eddie and Brandy reminisced off to the side, Larry and Diana couldn't help but imagine this is how it was supposed to be—their adult son with a woman he could love and who could love him back. This might have been their daughter-in-law, the mother of their grandchildren, and Diana could call up Eddie and say, "Hey, what are your plans for the weekend? You want to come over and have a barbecue? Bring the kids, or let me keep the kids this weekend while you and your wife go someplace and have some freedom."

For those few hours they could pretend they were a family once more. Eddie felt he was no longer in prison. He was a free man among those who loved him. Larry and Diana had their son back, and he belonged to them, not the state of Florida.

At 3 P.M. the illusion ended and the visitors courtyard emptied. Larry and Diana put their son back inside the box, slipped inside their rental car, and drove back to Orlando with Brandy.

On the way back to his cell, trying to keep the emotion inside from spilling out of his eyes, Eddie learned that while he was enjoying himself in the visitors courtyard, a man he worked with in PRIDE had died of a heart attack in the rec yard. The man's death awoke in Eddie, just now beginning to feel his own mortality, his greatest fear: that before his sentence was up, he might die alone, in prison, far from his family.

Clifford Barth

On the first weekend in October, the sidewalks and curbs of the main street start to fill with people carrying camp chairs and blankets in preparation for the parade of horses and cowboy hats leading to the fairgrounds for the Northwest Florida Championship Rodeo. In the hundred-year-old feed store there's a circle of worn-out office chairs where the old-timers still congregate to complain about the government and the weather. Across the street is the tent of the Sons of the Confederacy, selling Rebel flags, T-shirts, and bumper stickers that say "Confederate by Choice, Union by Force." The town is just rural enough to feel western, and near enough to Alabama to be southern.

The town is one mile from Holmes Correctional Institution, the prison where Cliff spent eight and a half years of his life sentence. He never set foot in the Florida town that, every time he heard its name, reminded him of the boy responsible for his imprisonment: Bonifay.

Holmes is where Cliff grew from a young adult into a middle-aged man in an open-air dorm with seventy other men. The long hair of his youth is gone. He wears it cut short to his scalp, military style, in an implicit acknowledgment of his beginning baldness. His face is narrow with a sharp, pointy chin. His lips are as thin as a scar, his brown eyes heavy-lidded.

A boy who, at the time of his conviction, had never been in jail before, Cliff has survived in prison by serving what amounts to solitary confinement. Keep to yourself. Don't make enemies. Don't make friends. The men in here, they aren't the kind of people you want to know. That's Cliff's philosophy of survival. He's a lone wolf in a pack-mentality predatory environment.

At Holmes he lifted weights, like the other prisoners, but always alone. He ran laps by himself around the track inside the chain-link fence bracketed top and bottom by coils of razor wire, and began his day with five hundred push-ups, along with leg dips and pull-ups.

In the dayroom, where the men crowded into the four metal benches and picnic table bolted to the floor and argued over what to watch on the TV mounted on the wall, Cliff was careful where he sat and whom he sat beside. He preferred the mornings, while the other inmates were eating, to have the dayroom to himself and watch the news.

The dorm was a large, open room with two rows of double bunks that ran along the side walls and three double bunks along the back wall with the four large windows. There were two rows of single bunks in the middle of the forty-two-by-sixty-five-foot room. A bulletin board on the front wall displayed the phone number for the prison rape hotline with instructions in English and Spanish.

The massive room was without air-conditioning. Large exhaust fans built into the walls blew the hot air around like a summer wind. Always wary, Cliff took showers to cool off in the summer heat of the Florida Panhandle. Twenty minutes after the cold shower he was sweating again, sitting shirtless on his bunk as a thin film of sweat covered his body.

On his bunk and in the dayroom with its bookshelf containing educational and religious materials, Cliff spent much of his time reading. He read in the morning, after the lights came on at 4:30 A.M. and when breakfast ended at 6 A.M. He read after they closed the workout yard at 10 A.M., and again before mail call at 3:15 P.M. He sometimes read between the master count at 9 P.M. and when they turned out the lights at 10 P.M. He read until his eyes hurt and his head ached.

In tiny, neat, printed letters, Cliff kept a log of the books he had read, entering another book title and author on the lined paper in his spiral notebook. Below John Grisham's *The Street Lawyer* he wrote down Harper Lee's *To Kill a Mockingbird*. The entries began with eight books by Dean Koontz, followed by Stephen King, Louis L'Amour, Jean Auel, and Thomas Harris. They continued through Mario Puzo,

Robert Ludlum, Herman Melville, Alexander Dumas, Jack London, Sir Walter Scott, Leo Tolstoy, Victor Hugo, and Fyodor Dostoyevsky. By 2011 the notebook numbered more than 717 books, giving Cliff the equivalent of a college degree in literature. The list was twenty-three pages long.

In his thirties, Cliff started working as a part-time helper for a heating and air-conditioning man who works inside the prison. But just as he was a teenager without ambitions, Cliff is a man without definite plans for the future. He doesn't focus on parole as something he can look forward to with any certainty. He doesn't invest any hope that when 2016 arrives he will be a free man. If it happens, he will deal with what comes next. If it doesn't, he will keep doing what he's been doing since 1991.

Prison gave Cliff little reason to plan for a future that might never occur. Inmates like Cliff are ineligible for opportunities to prepare for life outside prison. Since his imprisonment in 1991, Cliff qualified only for a GED class, which he completed in 1992. Because of his life sentence, all other requests for training or educational programs were denied. Over the years, Florida prisons have reduced and rationed rehabilitation programs. Those with five years or less to serve go to the front of the line for education and training. For lifers and those with long sentences, this is considered a waste of time and money. Cliff was told this bluntly in the written denial of his request to take a welding class in 1999: "My supervisor has denied your request for enrollment into the voc-welding class due to your long sentence."

In 2011, five years before he becomes eligible for parole, Cliff requested, and was granted, a transfer to Blackwater River Correctional Facility, a privately run prison in Milton. There were advantages to serving his time in Blackwater: the dorms are air-conditioned, the communal TVs are forty-two-inch flat-screens. There's ESPN and Netflix at Blackwater. But more important to Cliff, Blackwater offers educational opportunities not available at Holmes. Within three weeks of his transfer, Cliff was allowed to take a life-skills class that qualified him to enroll in vocational programs such as computer training and electrical classes.

Just as importantly, Blackwater moved Cliff closer to his relatives in Pensacola. Blackwater is farther than Holmes from Cliff's parents and sister, who live in Sevierville, Tennessee, but when they come to visit they can stay with family rather than in a motel room in Bonifay.

When he allows himself to imagine a future, Cliff thinks of family. He thinks of his niece, the girl he was babysitting the night of the murder, who is now an adult. Cliff imagines being a father someday. He thinks he would make a good one. Maybe with his own kids he can make up for the harm he caused his parents.

For a long time, Walter Barth blamed his wife for what happened to Cliff. And he blamed himself for not being there to keep Cliff away from Patrick Bonifay. Cliff's imprisonment nearly destroyed their marriage. Walt and Sheila didn't get divorced, but they've never been as close as they once were. They'll be watching TV together, and the loneliness will well up inside Walt and he will just get up and walk out of the room.

Walt changed after Cliff went to prison, and he never changed back. He used to be a carefree kind of guy. He's now a man soaked in sadness, regret, and sullenness.

Patrick Bonifay

In the 1990s, while still on death row, Patrick received a letter from a twenty-eight-year-old woman working as a special-education technician in San Diego, California, who found him on PrisonPenPals.com. He wrote her back: Why would you be interested in me? The woman, Saffiya, had received from her brother a book written by a Muslim man about his experiences in prison. The book, she wrote Patrick, compelled her to seek out a Muslim man on death row. Patrick and Saffiya traded letters for four years. Patrick learned that they both had converted to Islam in their twenties. Saffiya had grown up a Catholic girl from the Bronx. She spent four years in the Army, living out the military service that Patrick had aspired to. She'd had a bad childhood, same as him.

In 1999, Saffiya moved to Tampa to attend college at the University of South Florida and to be closer to Patrick. Early one morning in 2000, she drove the two hours and forty minutes to Raiford, where Patrick awaited his execution on death row. Without having met him, Saffiya felt she loved him and would someday marry him.

She wore pants, a flowered, earth-tone shirt, and a scarf the prison guards made her remove. They led her through a series of gates. Each time the gates clicked shut behind her, she shuddered. Inside the visitors room, they left her alone at a small round table. She sat there nervous, anxious, fearful, and wondering, second-guessing herself. *What am I doing here? Why do I love this man? What do I really know about him? What am I going to think of him when I see him?*

Patrick came into the room, dressed in his death-row orange shirt, starched white pants, tennis shoes, and the white kufi on his head. He walked up to the desk and showed his ID to the guard, who pointed a finger toward Saffiya at the table. He approached her with a big smile on his face. The doubts inside her head dissolved into one impulse: *I want to kiss him.*

Patrick reached for her hand, their fingers clasped, and then, for a brief moment, they kissed. His voice matched the sound of the words in his letters. She liked his smell. His face looked damn handsome to her: *He's some fine-ass white boy.*

They spent six hours talking that day. He told her about his childhood; she told him about her Africana studies at the University of South Florida. They talked about everything except the murder.

On the way out, to the sounds of the doors clanking and the locks clicking, she cried with the longing to take him with her, kiss him longer, hold him closer. In that visit, and the ones that followed every Saturday, Patrick left a package at the prison for her containing books on Islam, unsent letters, a kufi, and a plain white T-shirt of his that she slept with so his scent would be with her in her dreams.

A year later, Patrick and Saffiya symbolically became husband and wife, a married couple in the eyes of Islam. She took his last name and became Saffiya Musaaleh. In 2004, Patrick's mother, Theresa, asked Saffiya if she would adopt the son of Patrick's cousin, a girl who was about to lose her baby to the Department of Children and Families. Two weeks after the baby's birth, Saffiya became his mother. She gave him Nabiyl's last name, and in 2007 she officially adopted the boy. The boy called Patrick *Abu*, Arabic for *father*, but Saffiya did not add Patrick to the adoption papers as the boy's legal father.

By this time, Saffiya had become disillusioned with Patrick as a husband and a father. Their relationship was a roller-coaster ride of romance and recriminations, anger and forgiveness, love and hate. He admonished her for not being devout enough, not raising the boy correctly, not having a job, living on food stamps, not doing enough to help him raise the money he needed for the lawyer who could get him out of prison. She had helped him publish one of three books he wrote, an action novel in which a seventeen-year-old Muslim released from death row leads a band of Islamic warriors to avenge the slaughter of Muslim villagers in Uganda. In the unpublished sequel, the "Lions of Allah" take on Israeli special forces. When sales of the book failed to materialize, Patrick blamed Saffiya for rewriting the book to make it less raw and real.

After fifteen years with Patrick, Saffiya found herself in the same place as his mother—estranged by his anger and his demands for money to win his freedom. Saffiya stopped visiting Patrick, and he took her off his visiting list. She stopped accepting his calls, and he stopped writing her. She went from wondering if every time she visited him on death row it would be the last time she saw him alive to realizing that he might never again set foot outside prison. He would never understand what life was like for her, what it was like to be out of work and out of money, raising a five-year-old boy who needs you more than a man behind bars needs you.

In 2009, Patrick and Saffiya ended their relationship. She was forty-three. He was thirty-five.

On May 5, 2010, the U.S. Supreme Court did something it had never done before: it applied the Eighth Amendment prohibition against cruel and unusual punishment to something other than the death penalty. This time the defendants were two juveniles in Florida prisons, Terrance Graham and Joe Sullivan, who were sentenced to life without parole for non-homicide crimes. Terrance was seventeen when he was arrested for holding a gun to a man's head during a home invasion in Jacksonville. Joe was thirteen when he was arrested for raping a seventy-two-year-old woman.

At the time, 106 juveniles were serving life sentences in U.S. prisons with no chance of getting out. More than half of them, 77, were in Florida prisons. Patrick believed he belonged among them. His sentence for armed robbery, which was to take effect after he served his life sentence for murder, was for life without parole.

The case presented before the U.S. Supreme Court in *Graham v. Florida* was based on much of the same scientific evidence by many of the same researchers as in the *Roper v. Simmons* case five years before. On behalf of Terrance Graham, Jacksonville attorney Bryan Gowdy argued that a juvenile sentenced to life without parole was different from an adult who received the same sentence, because the juvenile was not yet a fully formed person. To sentence a teenager still capable of change, maturation, and rehabilitation to life in prison constituted cruel and unusual punishment.

"Sentencing an adolescent to life without any possibility of parole condemns him to die in prison and rejects any hope that he will change for the better," Gowdy said in his oral arguments before the Court. "This sentence, like the death penalty, cruelly ignores the inherent qualities of youth and the differences between adolescents and adults." Justices Anthony Kennedy, John Paul Stevens, Ruth Bader Ginsburg, Stephen Breyer, and Sonia Sotomayor agreed. The Court required that the juveniles serving life without parole be resentenced—raising the possibility that Patrick could live to see the outside of a prison one day.

In 2011, Patrick has been in prison more than half his life. Now middle-aged, he has lost the pudginess of his youth. His face is thin, his head shaved smooth beneath the knitted white kufi he wears at all times. Crow's-feet have begun to form around his eyes. His lips are narrow and his mouth pinched. His short frame is lean and hard. His arms and back are heavily inked with Islamic tattoos.

In 2009, eighteen years after his arrest in night school at Escambia High, Patrick received his GED. At the time he was an inmate at Wakulla Correctional Institution in Crawfordville, a two-hour drive from Georgiana, Alabama, where his parents had moved in 2001. They live in a small, blue frame house they bought with money the state gave them for their trailer, which stood in the way of a highway. The house is a few blocks from the railroad tracks and a weather-worn painted boxcar that declares Georgiana the birthplace of Hank Williams Sr. The walls of Theresa's dining room are decorated with photographs of Patrick as a child.

Every now and then, a thick envelope from Patrick will arrive in Theresa's mailbox. Each contains plans for Patrick's fantasy life of wealth and fame when he gets out of prison. He calls them his poor man's patents, trademarks, and copyrights, signed and dated and sealed inside the envelopes to prove that he had the idea before anyone else. There are the incorporation papers for Country Boy Enterprises and the reality TV show that Patrick describes with breathless enthusiasm: "You're going to see this on the Outdoor Channel. I've already got my trademarks mailed out and they're locked in already and the first one is called Ultimate Country Boy Challenge and you got a four-wheel truck with a four-wheeler in the back of it. It's a timed race. You take off and jump through the woods and fire trails and everything. This is major coverage. They've got helicopters in the air covering the front-runners. Major sponsorships. Alright, they take the truck out into the mud. They got to get the four-wheeler out of the truck and pull the truck out of the mud. The four-wheeler goes this a-way, down a trail. The truck goes this way. You got to jump out of the truck, out of the four-wheeler, run over to a station, pick up a bow, and you got to shoot the deer targets—Hoyt sponsors the bow area—and once they hit all the targets, you got to turn and they run into the river, dive into the river, they've got to swim down to where the canoes are, get into the canoe, paddle to another place, jump out and run over the mother of all obstacle courses and a one-point-five mile run to the finish line. Fifty thousand dollars cash. There is no second place."

The plans for Country Boy Enterprises' Ultimate Country Boy Challenge are stored with the other envelopes in a plastic filing box that Theresa keeps below her computer desk as a footrest.

. . .

Crain's Cemetery is a parched open graveyard of few trees at the end of the two-lane Trinity Baptist Church Road five miles outside Milton, a small town turning into a bedroom community twenty-three miles northeast of Pensacola. Families have taken to covering their sandy cemetery plots with gravel corralled by curb-like borders. Graves are decorated with ceramic doves and angels and deer, Mardi Gras beads, perfume bottles, toy trucks and motorcycles. Scenes of men fishing for bass or pickups towing travel trailers are etched on granite tombstones. There are elaborate headstones and statuary gardens, but there are also grave markers with names and dates scratched with sticks into wet concrete or painted on rocks or carved onto a board with a wood-burning tool.

Two decades after his death, Billy Wayne Coker rests beneath a concrete slab in the center of Crain's Cemetery, his grave identified by an aluminum marker the size of an index card with raised letters and numbers slid one by one into rails to form three lines of type:

Billy W. Coker
May 12, 1954
Jan. 27, 1991

Coda

In a letter sent to Sandra Faye Coker from the Escambia County Jail following his conviction on August 28, 1991, eighteen-year-old Eddie Fordham wrote about why he thought her husband, Billy Wayne Coker, was killed.

"Mrs. Coker, I have a theory. I don't personally know Robin Archer, Daniel Wells, Edward Byrd, and hardly did I know Patrick Bonifay. However, through reliable sources, I've been confirmed that Trout Auto Parts was a '*Drug* Parts Store.' I've learned that Mr. Wells and Mr. Byrd are both drug users and dealers. Both have worked for 'Trout Drug Parts' for several years and that Mr. Archer was one of their co-conspirators. At some point and time, Mr. Archer was fired by his boss, but Mr. Archer did not care, because he was still partners with Mr. Byrd and could still launder drugs and money through Trout Auto as a cover up. It was the perfect conspiracy. This is why Mr. Archer never bothered getting another job. He suddenly became Trout Auto Parts 'Outside-Inside' man. He was on the outside making deals, but was actually on the inside of everything that was going on. I feel that since your husband was such a Christian man, according to my uncle, that Mr. Coker stepped across what was going on at Trout Auto Parts. As a result, Mr. Byrd, Mr. Wells, and Mr. Archer became nervous at your husbands knowledge of this illegal conspiracy. Mrs. Coker, I may spend twenty-five (25) years in prison, but I will continue believing that since Robin Archer was not any longer working for Trout there would be no speculation on his part of the murder and therefore Mr. Archer was the one the three decided on to eliminate their problem. They were making so much money that a human life did not matter or who they had to use to do it.

"I now believe that on Friday night January 25, 1991, Mr. Bonifay had me take him to Trout Auto Parts to talk to Mr. Wells about how to get Mr. Coker over to the W. Street store, because it was the one with the parts window and the easiest to get rid of someone and make it look like a robbery. At that time, Mr. Wells told Patrick Bonifay that he would call in sick Saturday and get Billy Wayne Coker (who needed the money) to work in his place that night. The night your husband was killed.

"I believe in this theory because Robin Archer has told me that he went to Trout around 10:00 or 10:30 pm that Saturday night with Edward Byrd and he (Robbin) saw your husband working. He went there (my opinion) with Edward Byrd to verify for Patrick Bonifay that Mr. Coker *was* working. If Mr. Archer had wanted Mr. Wells killed, then he would have contacted Patrick Bonifay and would have told him that Daniel Wells was *not* working and to not go through with it."

Homicide investigator Tom O'Neal and Prosecutor Michael Patterson heard the same theory—and dismissed it. They believed that Robin Archer was dealing drugs from Trout Auto and that the loss of that source of income—not a menial, low-paying job—was the motivation for his hiring Patrick Bonifay to kill Daniel Wells a year after his firing. But they found no evidence that Wells was involved with Archer and his co-worker Edward Byrd in the murder of Billy Wayne Coker.

Eddie's theory, however, answers several problems with the mistaken-identity-murder-for-hire story that convicted Patrick, Eddie, Cliff and Archer. If Wells was not the intended victim, it explains why Patrick approached the window Friday night without a fully loaded gun. If Wells was involved in the plot to kill Coker with Archer and Patrick, it explains why the description he gave of the boy who approached the window Friday night looks like Clifford Barth and not Patrick Bonifay. Barth had never been to Trout Auto before, never got out of the car that Friday night. Wells stood face-to-face with Patrick that night, yet the sketch looks nothing like him. Patrick could have provided Wells with a picture of Cliff in advance of the murder.

If Wells was involved in Coker's murder, it also explains why the needle moved on two questions during his polygraph test: "Regarding Wayne's death, are you deliberately withholding any information about it?" and "Did you know about the robbery before it happened?"

Moreover, Tim Eaton testified that Wells had nothing to do with the firing of Robin Archer and that Archer, who kept coming by the store, never seemed too upset about having lost his job.

Finally, there's Billy Wayne Coker himself. Prior to taking the job with Trout Auto Parts, Coker was a patrolman for about five years with the police department in Jackson, Mississippi. The theory that Coker, not Wells, was the target all along contends that Coker knew there was drug dealing going on at Trout, that he was not a part of it, and that he presented a threat to the dealers because he might inform the police.

Robin Archer, in his trial and appeals, denied hiring Patrick to kill anyone at Trout Auto Parts. Patrick continues to insist that it was a botched robbery, not a contract murder.

Sandra Coker never replied to Eddie's letter.

Acknowledgments

I would like to thank Jacob Levenson, Tom French, and Leslie Rubinkowski for their insight and guidance; Patsy Sims for her patience and understanding; and Mick Lochridge, Gene Kruckemyer, and both Bill Kunerths for their astute eye for my errors, omissions, and typographical miscues. I also owe a word of thanks to the Florida Department of Corrections. Without the cooperation of Patrick Bonifay, Eddie Fordham, and Clifford Barth, this book could not have been written.

Notes on Sources

This book is a work of creative nonfiction. Everything written is based on interviews, letters, court documents, trial transcripts, newspaper and magazine articles, books, research papers, photographs, and firsthand reporting. It attempts to stitch together the truth based on contradictory stories of what happened before, during, and after the night of January 26, 1991. While this story may differ from the versions told by Patrick Bonifay, Eddie Fordham and Clifford Barth, nothing in this book is fictional. All interviews cited were conducted by the author.

Prologue

Patrick Bonifay stepped slowly: Patrick Bonifay interview, September 25, 2009.

Robin Lee Archer had set it up: Patrick Bonifay police statement, February 11, 1991.

Patrick didn't even care much for Eddie: Patrick Bonifay interview, January 30, 2009.

Patrick thought Cliff was alright: Patrick Bonifay interview, October 17, 2008.

When Patrick called the night before: Clifford Barth testimony, Bonifay trial, July 15, 1991, p. 294.

Eddie and Cliff were almost strangers: Eddie Fordham interview, July 17, 2009.

It was a menial, low-paying job: Tom O'Neal interview, September 30, 2009; Bonifay testimony, July 19, 1991, p. 301.

He blamed Wells for his firing: Daniel Wells polygraph statement, January 30, 1991, p. 5.

Patrick was desperate: Patrick Bonifay interview, September 9, 2009.

As he approached the front of Trout Auto Parts: Patrick Bonifay interview, September 9, 2009.

Man, I am this far away from making it, Patrick thought: Patrick Bonifay interview, September 9, 2009.

Patrick tried to look calm: Patrick Bonifay interview, September 9, 2009.

"I want you to check: Wells testimony, Bonifay trial, July 15, 1991, p. 210.

Patrick slipped off his right glove: Wells testimony, July 15, 1991, p. 210.

Wells, who was off to the side: Wells testimony, Bonifay retrial, October 17, 1994, p. 288.

Something about the boy at the window: Wells testimony, Bonifay trial, July 15, 1991, p. 209.

"I don't have it," he said: Wells testimony, Bonifay trial, July 15, 1991, p. 210.

A surge of relief flooded over him: Patrick Bonifay interview, September 9, 2009.

"Everything's cool": Eddie Fordham interview, November 21, 2008.

Chapter 1. The Boys

I am sick of this shit: Patrick Bonifay letter, March 21, 2010.

He didn't like the feeling of being confined: Patrick Bonifay interview, September 12, 2008.

But that wasn't Brownsville: *Pensacola News Journal*, November 20, 1997; author's observations.

Those who remained in the early 1990s: *Pensacola News Journal*, February 16, 1991.

As soon as he was old enough for school: Escambia County school records; Theresa Crenshaw interview, September 26, 2009.

Theresa didn't tell the doctors: Crenshaw interview, September 26, 2009.

Sometimes Howard's cousin Robin Archer: Bonifay testimony, Robin Archer trial excerpt, July 16, 1991, p. 8.

Even Patrick's father lived with them: Crenshaw testimony, Bonifay retrial, October 19, 1994, p. 352.

In Theresa's trailer, dinner was grab a plate: Patrick Bonifay interview, October 17, 2008.

From the front yard of his grandfather's house: Patrick Bonifay interview, October 17, 2008.

He saw something of himself in the boy: Crenshaw interview, September 26, 2009.

In his grandfather's house: Patrick Bonifay interview, October 17, 2008.

But there were problems in James Scarbrough's house: Crenshaw interview, September 26, 2009.

Patrick lived inside the realm: Patrick Bonifay interview, October 17, 2008; Crenshaw interview, September 26, 2009.

Something inside Patrick: Patrick Bonifay interview, October 17, 2008.

The day he swallowed his sister's pills: Patrick Bonifay interview, November 14, 2008.

Kelly Bland, Patrick's best friend: Bonifay letter, October 29, 2008.

His grandfather thought Patrick: Patrick Bonifay interview, November 14, 2008.

The next night, Scarbrough ripped into Patrick: Bonifay letter, October 29, 2008.

"Pop, you don't understand, man": Bonifay interview, November 14, 2008.

"Man," Patrick said to Howard: Bonifay letter, October 29, 2008.

Theresa and Howard watched: Crenshaw interview, September 26, 2009.

He waited for Scott to come take him away: Patrick Bonifay interview, November 14, 2008.

he went to work for a drug dealer: Patrick Bonifay interview, November 14, 2008.

I'm going to die out here: Patrick Bonifay interview, October 17, 2008.

Toward the end of the summer: Larry E. Fordham Jr., "Fast Eddie and the Crossroads of Choice: A True Story for Teens," copyright 1991–2007, p. 8.

close enough to smell the scent: Fordham, "Fast Eddie," 10.

"Eddie Fordham," C.J. said: Fordham, "Fast Eddie," 10.

It's always my fault, Eddie thought: Fordham, "Fast Eddie," 13.

Eddie was his mother's miracle baby: Eddie Fordham interview, November 21, 2008.

Pensacola missed the rapid population growth: Pensacola historian Earle Bowden interview, March 18, 2011.

a shovel full of dirt could unearth: Eddie Fordham interview, August 27, 2009.

After three years in Pensacola: Eddie Fordham interview, November 21, 2008.

At eighteen, Eddie craved kicks and acceptance: Eddie Fordham interview, November 21, 2008.

It made him feel unpopular: Eddie Fordham interview, August 29, 2009.

The teenage need to belong: Eddie Fordham interview, November 21, 2008.

"You're sweating," Eddie said: Fordham, "Fast Eddie," 16.

"I don't remember asking anyone: Fordham, "Fast Eddie," 17.

"It's Eddie's mom: Fordham, "Fast Eddie," 22.

Eddie could feel the adrenaline kick in: Fordham, "Fast Eddie," 23.

They left me! They shit on me: Eddie Fordham interview, December 9, 2010.

George Wynne pulled the pickup behind: Clifford Barth interview, October 2, 2009.

It was late at night on December 22: Escambia County Sheriff's Department report, March 6, 1991.

I can't believe I'm doing this: Clifford Barth interview, October 2, 2009.

Cliff had felt adrift since he arrived: Clifford Barth interview, March 9, 2009.

Loyalty to country didn't necessarily translate: Bowden interview, March 18, 2001.

In its geography, history, and heritage: Bowden interview, March 18, 2011.

Pensacola's attachment to the rest of Florida: Bowden interview, March 18, 2011.

Over its history, Pensacola has drawn Greeks: Bowden interview, March 18, 2011.

On Christmas Day in 1984: *Washington Post*, January 6, 1985.

the Gulf War put the city's pride: *Pensacola News Journal*, January 28, 1991.

Eddie Fordham's parents made the papers: *Pensacola News Journal*, September 21, 1990.

Other kids saw Cliff as a headbanger stoner: Patrick Bonifay interview, September 12, 2008.

It felt good to have a cousin like Bland: Clifford Barth interview, October 2, 2009.

Bland looked tough, but Patrick was tough: Clifford Barth interview, March 9, 2009.

He had spent six months in boot camp: Patrick Bonifay interview, January 30, 2009.

It was hard for Cliff to tell fact from fiction: Clifford Barth interview, March 9, 2009.

He'd screwed a hundred women: Patrick Bonifay interview, November 14, 2008.

So it always came as something of a surprise: Clifford Barth interview, October 2, 2009.

One day Cliff went to the mall: Clifford Barth letter, August 15, 2009.

Or following Patrick into a house: David Kelly Bland statement, February 15, 1991, p. 3.

Once they were inside, Cliff felt: Clifford Barth interview, October 2, 2009.

Eric took a couple of quick steps: Barth letter, July 15, 2009.

in the back of the truck: Escambia County Sheriff's Department report, March 6, 1991.

Chapter 2. Trout Auto

The sense of relief that came over Patrick: Patrick Bonifay interview, September 9, 2009.
implanted teeth he liked to show off: Crenshaw interview, September 26, 2009.
He had no place of his own: Presentence Investigation report, August 14, 1991.
Trout Auto Parts was a family-owned chain: Timothy Allen Eaton testimony, Eddie Fordham trial, August 27, 1991, p. 124.
would slip himself a twenty: Wells polygraph statement, January 30, 1991, p. 4.
Other employees, like Archer, made their money selling drugs: Bonifay testimony, July 19, 1991, p. 301.
Archer was an indifferent, surly worker: Eaton deposition, July 15, 1991, pp. 1–6.
Archer acted like he was the boss: Wells deposition, July 15, 1991, p. 6.
He knew that when Archer worked at the Ensley store: Eaton deposition, July 15, 1991, p. 6.
Archer didn't make a scene: Eaton deposition, July 15, 1991, p. 9.
"You want to know how?": Wells testimony, Bonifay trial, July 15, 1991, p. 215.
Inside Patrick's bedroom: Patrick Bonifay interview, September 9, 2009.
I can do this, Patrick thought: Patrick Bonifay interview, September 9, 2009.
"Alright, alright, already," Patrick snapped: Patrick Bonifay interview, April 5, 2010.

Chapter 3. The Murder

"I need you to come pick me up": Eddie Fordham interview, November 21, 2008.
Eddie envied Patrick: Eddie Fordham interview, November 21, 2008.
Saturday was starting to feel like Friday night: Eddie Fordham interview, August 29, 2009.
"I talked to Nikki and Rachael: Eddie Fordham interview, November 21, 2008.
Eddie got ready for his date with Nikki: Eddie Fordham interview, January 29, 2010.
"You got a ski mask?": Eddie Fordham interview, November 21, 2008.
Eddie was having problems with his Mustang: Eddie Fordham interview, November 21, 2008.
"Naw, man, what's really going on: Eddie Fordham interview, November 21, 2008.
"What do you need bullets for?": Eddie Fordham interview, November 21, 2008.
Eddie pulled into the Kmart: Eddie Fordham police statement, February 11, 1991; Eddie Fordham interview, November 21, 2008.
I'm not in jail: Barth letter, November 3, 2009.
Cliff spent the day doing chores: Barth letter, November 3, 2009.
He had rescued her: Barth letter, May 31, 2009.
Cliff was babysitting: Barth letter, November 3, 2009.
We're going back to rob Trout Auto: Clifford Barth interview, March 9, 2009.
Cliff tried to convince himself: Barth letter, November 3, 2009.
Cliff smoked a little weed: Barth letter, November 3, 2009.
Patrick loaded the bullets: Clifford Barth interview, October 2, 2009; Barth letter, November 18, 2009.

Why does Patrick need a fully loaded gun?: Clifford Barth interview, October 2, 2009; Barth letter, November 18, 2009.

The gun Kelly gave Patrick: Patrick Bonifay interview, October 17, 2009.

Patrick had to pick through an assortment: Patrick Bonifay interview, September 29, 2009.

We are not going to do this: Barth letter, November 18, 2009.

It should be George Wynne driving: George Wynne deposition, July 16, 1991, p. 17.

George and Patrick had lived together: Wynne deposition, July 16, 1991, p. 5.

"Don't do this. It's crazy, it's stupid": Wynne deposition, July 16, 1991, p. 17.

Patrick saw in Kelly a reflection of himself: Patrick Bonifay interview, January 30, 2009.

Patrick dismissed Eddie's taste in music: Patrick Bonifay interview, April 5, 2010.

that song Patrick liked to listen to: Eddie Fordham interview, November 21, 2008.

Get this crazy shit over: Patrick Bonifay interview, September 9, 2009.

Eddie sat behind the wheel: Eddie Fordham interview, November 21, 2008.

He felt like he was inside an episode: Eddie Fordham interview, November 21, 2008.

I'm in. I'm cool. I'm one of them: Eddie Fordham interview, August 29, 2009.

Eddie could see the clerk inside the store: Eddie Fordham police statement, February 11, 1991.

Inside the excitement was a twinge of guilt: Eddie Fordham interview, January 29, 2010.

For most of his life, Coker: Sandra Faye Coker deposition, October 22, 1993, p. 13.

Before he landed the job with Trout: Wells polygraph statement, January 30, 1991, p. 2.

Buddy Turner . . . called Coker around 2:30: Wells polygraph statement, January 30, 1991, p. 6.

Coker's kids called him Uncle Dan: Wells polygraph statement, January 30, 1991, p. 2.

his face . . . was stubble: crime scene photo.

Sandra and Wayne kissed before he left: Pensacola News Journal, September 21, 1991.

Wayne smoked a cigarette and drank a can of Coke: Escambia Sheriff's Department crime scene report, January 27, 1991; Billy Wayne Coker autopsy report, February 29, 1991.

doubt competed with determination: Patrick Bonifay interview, April 5, 2010.

"I'll be right with you": Bonifay testimony, Robin Archer trial excerpt, July 16, 1991, p. 5.

This is it. Do it!: Patrick Bonifay interview, September 9, 2009.

the gunshot was so loud: Clifford Barth interview, March 9, 2009; Barth letter, November 18, 2009.

"He did it": Barth letter, February 27, 2010.

He felt his heartbeat accelerate: Barth letter, November 18, 2009.

Patrick was halfway through the window: Clifford Barth interview, October 2, 2009.

He was halfway in before he realized: Barth letter, November 18, 2009.

Cliff felt his vision narrow: Barth letter, November 18, 2009.

"I can't cut the locks off, Pat!": Patrick Bonifay interview, April 5, 2010; Barth letter, February 27, 2010.

Cliff couldn't feel the gun: Barth letter, November 18, 2009.

"Please, don't shoot me again": Barth testimony, Robin Archer trial, July 17, 1991, p. 68.

The sound of Coker's voice competed: Barth letter, November 18, 2009.

"Pat, he's not dead," Cliff said: Patrick Bonifay interview, April 5, 2010.

"Shut the fuck up: Barth testimony, Bonifay trial, July 15, 1991, p. 29.

In Patrick's mind: Patrick Bonifay interview, April 5, 2010.

Eddie was getting nervous: Eddie Fordham interview, November 21, 2008.

"Let's go! Let's go!": Eddie Fordham interview, August 29, 2009.

Cliff counted out the money: Eddie Fordham police statement, February 11, 1991.

"There was a man on the phone: Eddie Fordham testimony, Fordham trial, August 28, 1991, p. 90.

Patrick dumped the checks: Eddie Fordham testimony, Fordham trial, August 28, 1991, p. 90.

The teens went upstairs to Eddie's bedroom: Eddie Fordham interview, November 21, 2008.

"Do you want to know what happened: Eddie Fordham interview, November 21, 2008.

That's the end of my life: Eddie Fordham interview, November 21, 2008.

Chapter 4. The Arrest

O'Neal rolled out of bed: Tom O'Neal interview, September 30, 2009.

Walker was in his mother's house: Jerry Walker deposition, May 16, 1991.

"Sheriff's communications": transcript of Walker's call, January 25, 1991.

Seventeen minutes into Sunday: Van Weeks testimony, Fordham trial, August 27, 1991, p. 2.

a man was facedown, blood spreading: crime scene photo.

the phone's receiver dangling from the counter: Escambia County Sheriff's Department death scene investigation report, January 27, 1991.

By the time O'Neal arrived: Death scene investigation report, January 27, 1991.

The store was old and cluttered: crime scene photos.

O'Neal examined the body without touching it: O'Neal interview, September 30, 2009.

Coker's shaggy brown hair: crime scene photo.

O'Neal could see obvious signs: O'Neal interview, September 30, 2009.

a pair of black leather gloves: Death scene investigation report, January 27, 1991.

Sandra was up: Sandra Faye Coker interview, April 8, 2010.

"I know this must be about my husband: Coker interview, April 8, 2010.

In Sandra's mind: Coker interview, April 8, 2010.

"Momma, where's Daddy at?: Coker interview, April 8, 2010.

My gosh, Sandra thought: Coker interview, April 8, 2010.

It was 5 A.M. when O'Neal: O'Neal interview, September 30, 2009.

O'Neal began with a logical suspect: O'Neal interview, September 30, 2009.

Wells dreamed of leaving: Wells polygraph report, January 30, 1991, p. 6.

He was nervous and emotional: Wells polygraph report, January 30, 1991, p. 2.

"I feel guilty: Wells polygraph report, January 30, 1991, p. 5.

it was probably Robbie: Wells polygraph report, January 30, 1991, p. 5.

Wells then reiterated: Wells polygraph report, January 30, 1991, p. 7.

Wells had thought about calling the police: Wells polygraph report, January 30, 1991, p. 8.

The polygraph did not completely exonerate: Wells polygraph report, January 30, 1991, p. 8.

O'Neal was also hearing rumors: O'Neal interview, September 30, 2009.

In the bedroom closet of Eddie Fordham's room: Eddie Fordham letter, March 17, 2010.

Patrick was spending money too: Rachael Byrd interview, April 7, 2010.

Rachael thought of it as something: Byrd interview, October 1, 2009.

He had told her he knew a way to get $50,000: Byrd interview, October 1, 2009.

Eddie wore the wet suit once: Eddie Fordham letter, March 17, 2010.

He concentrated instead on graduating: Eddie Fordham interview, August 27, 2009.

Patrick was still calling Eddie: Eddie Fordham interview, December 19, 2008.

Eddie took Nikki out to dinner: Eddie Fordham letter, March 17, 2010.

"You should give it to her now": Eddie Fordham letter, March 17, 2010.

Patrick was emotional and weepy: Jody Bonifay interview, September 27, 2009.

she knew something was wrong: Crenshaw interview, September 26, 2009.

He gave her money: Patrick Bonifay interview, January 30, 2009.

She was afraid to ask: Crenshaw interview, September 26, 2009.

Patrick was at war within himself: Patrick Bonifay interview, November 14, 2008.

he asked Kelly to put some fear: David Kelly Bland deposition, May 19, 1991, p. 10.

Rachael and Patrick went to Johnson's Beach: Patrick Bonifay interview, April 5, 2010.

All he could think about: Patrick Bonifay interview, April 2, 2010.

In the days after the murder: Clifford Barth interview, October 2, 2009; Barth letter, March 28, 2010.

he sat sweating, his heart pounding: Barth letter, March 28, 2010.

Coker's murder had Pensacola on edge: *Pensacola News Journal*, January 29, 30, 1991.

Ted Bundy, on his way out of Florida: *Pensacola Journal*, February 18, 1979; Pensacola Police Department history, www.pensacolapolice.com/details.asp?pid=2482.

In 1983 the owner of a beauty shop: Chris Anderson and Sharon McGehee, *Bodies of Evidence: The True Story of Judias Buenoano Florida's Serial Murderess* (Secaucus, N.J.: Carol Publishing Group, 1991), 12–20.

In 1989, Timothy Robinson joined Judy: Florida Department of Corrections, www.dc.state.fl.us/activeinmates/detail.

The drawing appeared: *Pensacola News Journal*, February 7, 1991.

It never occurred to him that the killer: O'Neal interview, September 30, 2009.

On O'Neal's desk: Bonifay court records.

Since the murder: O'Neal interview, September 30, 2009.

Patrick called Morris: Jennifer Tatum Morris statement, February 14, 1991.

"Well, I did it": Morris statement, February 14, 1991.

"He killed him because the man saw his face": Morris statement, February 14, 1991.

"He shot the guy": Bland statement, February 11, 1991.

Martin told O'Neal that he knew Eddie: Tom Martin interview, March 12, 2009.

Eddie got out of school early: Escambia High Assistant Principal Larry Huntley interview, March 10, 2009.

He'd been at the part-time job for about a year: Parole and Probation Services Presentence Investigation report, August 14, 1991, p. 9.

Eddie looked up to see two men: Eddie Fordham interview, December 19, 2008.

Eddie was not surprised: Eddie Fordham interview, December 19, 2008.

"Where's my father?": Eddie Fordham interview, December 19, 2008.

"Look, Eddie, we know that you're the least involved: Eddie Fordham interview, December 19, 2008; Martin interview, March 12, 2009.

"Wait until we get to the office": Martin deposition, May 2, 1991, p. 6.

He'd been there before: Eddie Fordham interview, December 19, 2008.

He didn't want to take Eddie into an interrogation room: O'Neal interview, September 30, 2009.

"You want to call your parents?": Martin interview, March 12, 2009.

Eddie didn't like him: Eddie Fordham interview, December 19, 2008.

"I want to make that phone call": Eddie Fordham interview, December 19, 2008.

Where's my dad?: Eddie Fordham interview, December 19, 2008.

Eddie looked like one of those kids: O'Neal interview, September 30, 2009.

That's why they picked him up first: O'Neal interview, September 30, 2009.

O'Neal pulled a chair up next to Eddie: O'Neal interview, September 30, 2009.

"I know this is going to be rough on you: *Larry Edwin Fordham v. State of Florida,* First Circuit Appeal, September 3, 1996, p. 5.

Eddie's version of what happened: audio transcript of Fordham's statement, February 11, 1991.

O'Neal was thinking: O'Neal interview, September 30, 2009.

He doesn't get it: O'Neal interview, September 30, 2009.

Eddie was shocked: Eddie Fordham interview, December 19, 2008.

After he took off his clothes, Eddie folded them: Eddie Fordham interview, November 6, 2009.

Maybe, he thought, it means "Save for One Hour.": Eddie Fordham interview, November 6, 2009.

As O'Neal was questioning Eddie: Diana Fordham testimony, Fordham evidentiary hearing on post-conviction relief, July 1, 1997, p. 13.

"Don't we have any say about the matter?": Diana Fordham testimony, Fordham evidentiary hearing, July 1, 1997, p. 23.

"He's eighteen. He belongs to the state now": Diana Fordham testimony, Fordham evidentiary hearing, July 1, 1997, p. 23; Diana Fordham interview, March 7, 2009.

"Well, he made his bed, he can sleep in it": Larry Fordham Sr. testimony, Fordham evidentiary hearing, July 1, 1997, p. 34.

He immediately regretted his words: Larry Fordham Sr. testimony, Fordham evidentiary hearing, July 1, 1997, p. 33.

he needed to move fast: O'Neal interview, September 30, 2009.

On the way to the high school: Allan Cotton deposition, May 3, 1991, pp. 9–10.

Cotton and Martin walked past the concrete green gator: author's observation.

Patrick thought this was a good thing: Patrick Bonifay interview, April 5, 2010.

I'm done. My life is over: Patrick Bonifay interview, September 9, 2009.

This kid's cocky: O'Neal interview, September 30, 2009.

"Look, we know what happened: O'Neal interview, September 30, 2009.

O'Neal found Patrick's remark as amazing: O'Neal interview, September 30, 2009.

But Martin and O'Neal knew: Martin interview, March 12, 2009.

In O'Neal's mind: O'Neal interview, September 30, 2009.

Patrick's mind was racing: Patrick Bonifay interview, April 5, 2010.

They're going to kill me: Patrick Bonifay interview, September 9, 2009.

Patrick believed that the only thing: Patrick Bonifay interview, April 5, 2010.

"Would you in just your own words: audiotape of Bonifay's statement, February 11, 1991.

O'Neal took notes as Patrick talked: Bonifay arrest documents.

He had a clear mental picture of Patrick: O'Neal interview, September 30, 2009.

After Patrick finished his confession: Cotton testimony, Bonifay trial, July 15, 1991, p. 279.

Archer had started drinking at twelve: Parole and Probation Services Presentence Investigation report, August 14, 1991, p. 8.

Archer's '85 Nissan pickup matched: Jody Bonifay interview, April 8, 2010.

"You don't have anything on me. I've got an alibi": O'Neal deposition, June 7, 1991, p. 19.

Cliff's mother, Sheila, was watching TV: Sheila Barth interview, May 7, 2009.

"Is Cliff here?": Sheila Barth interview, May 7, 2009.

Sheila felt her heart stop: Sheila Barth interview, May 7, 2009.

He had expected this day: Clifford Barth interview, October 2, 2009.

Cliff stopped chewing: Barth letter, April 5, 2009.

"I want to tell you the truth": O'Neal interview, September 30, 2009.

"No," O'Neal replied, "not at this point": Sheila Barth interview, May 7, 2009.

During the drive to the sheriff's department: Barth letter, November 18, 2009.

It's over now: Barth letter, November 18, 2009.

I didn't kill anybody: Clifford Barth interview, October 2, 2009.

"I didn't pull the trigger": Barth statement, February 11, 1991, p. 5.

He was exhausted and exhilarated: O'Neal interview, September 30, 2009.

the courthouse was a no-nonsense building: Martin Levin interview, March 4, 2011.

good at seeing things in straight lines: P. Michael Patterson interview, September 29, 2009.

Patterson felt he could convict: Patterson interview, September 29, 2009.

Chapter 5. Act Negates Age

On the evening of March 6, 1978, two teenagers: Fox Butterfield, *All God's Children: The Bosket Family and the American Tradition of Violence* (New York: Vintage Books, 1995), 209.

In his world, violence was a code of conduct: Butterfield, *All God's Children*, 207.

"Didn't I say get your ass over here?": Butterfield, *All God's Children*, 210.

and this time he had a gun: Butterfield, *All God's Children*, 210.

If he's not dead, he's going to cause me a problem: Butterfield, *All God's Children*, 211.

"I killed a motherfucker," he said, laughing: Butterfield, *All God's Children*, 211.

It felt like no big deal: Butterfield, *All God's Children*, 211.

three inches from the man's head: Butterfield, *All God's Children*, 215.

Whatever empathy his might once have had: Butterfield, *All God's Children*, 215.

Shock turned to outrage: Butterfield, *All God's Children*, 226.

In response, Governor Hugh Carey: Butterfield, *All God's Children*, 227.

Three years later, the Sunshine State joined the wave: "The Florida Experiment: Transferring Power from Judges to Prosecutors," *Criminal Justice Magazine,* Spring 2000, 1.

juvenile justice system created by the Progressives: The Chicago Juvenile Court Movement in the 1890s, Elizabeth J. Clapp, University of Leicester, March 17, 1995, www.le.ac.uk/hi/teaching/papers/clapp1.html.

replaced parole with mandatory sentences: Florida Department of Corrections, Sentencing Guidelines 1995–96 Annual Report.

Chapter 6. The Trial

Patterson embraced the power of his position: Patterson interview, September 29, 2009.

the guardian of justice: Patterson interview, September 29, 2009.

The only person on death row: www.floridacapitalcases.state.fl.us/Enewsletter/Lecroy.pdf, p. 1.

last time Florida executed a teenager: Florida Department of Corrections, Death Row Fact Sheet, www.dc.state.fl.us/oth/deathrow/index.html.

the act alone turned Patrick from a boy into a man: Patterson interview, September 29, 2009.

night of the Trout Auto murder: Diana Fordham interview, March 7, 2009.

Fordhams had trouble finding a lawyer: Larry Fordham Sr. interview, March 7, 2009.

Collier was typical of a breed of transplanted: Bowden interview, March 18, 2011.

"Mother-in-law of the U.S. Navy": Bowden interview, March 18, 2011.

Born in Demopolis, Alabama, Collier trained as a pilot: Earle Bowden, "Lacey Collier: From Navy Skies to Federal Bench," *Pensacola Magazine,* March 1993, 12–13.

some defense attorneys complained: www.therobingroom.com.

Even experienced defense attorneys knew: Levin interview, March 4, 2011.

Eddie ended up with Assistant Public Defender: Elton Killam interview, September 25, 2009.

Killam felt he was doing a former classmate a favor: Killam interview, September 25, 2009.

Killam also knew Patterson from their days growing up: Killam interview, September 25, 2009.

As Killam saw it: Killam interview, September 25, 2009.

Eddie felt intimidated: Eddie Fordham interview, January 29, 1010.

Eddie felt like a sheep: Eddie Fordham interview, January 29, 1010.

"The truth will set you free": Eddie Fordham interview, November 21, 2008.

Patterson looked annoyed: Eddie Fordham interview, January 29, 2010.

Eddie felt Patterson didn't want the truth: Eddie Fordham interview, November 21, 2008.

"I'm sorry, but I cannot testify: Eddie Fordham interview, November 21, 2008.

Patterson didn't get what he hoped for from Eddie: Eddie Fordham interview, January 29, 2010.

Patterson had gone into the meeting thinking Eddie: Patterson interview, September 29, 2009.

This wasn't the first time the boy had been in trouble: Eddie Fordham interview, December 19, 2008.

Patterson didn't believe a word of it: Patterson interview, September 29, 2009.

Eddie didn't appear scared or intimidated to Patterson: Patterson interview, September 29, 2009.

Patterson told Eddie: Patterson interview, September 29, 2009.

Eddie was under the mistaken impression: Patterson interview, September 29, 2009.

Eddie didn't get it: Patterson interview, September 29, 2009.

Their encounter was disastrous: Patterson interview, September 29, 2009.

Seeing his lawyer and the prosecutor together: Clifford Barth interview, October 2, 2009.

he offered his client some legal advice: Clifford Barth interview, October 2, 2009.

Cliff felt confused and uneasy: Clifford Barth interview, October 2, 2009.

In return for Cliff's cooperation: Clifford Barth interview, October 2, 2009.

I really don't need you: Patterson interview, September 29, 2009.

I'm seventeen years old: Clifford Barth interview, October 2, 2009.

Patterson offered one more assurance: Clifford Barth interview, October 2, 2009.

Cliff's attorney was never present: Clifford Barth interview, October 2, 2009.

Patterson liked Cliff the moment he met him: Patterson interview, September 29, 2009.

To Patterson, they were all: Patterson interview, September 29, 2009.

The sky was partly cloudy: Pensacola News Journal, July 16, 1991.

He wore a plain white shirt: Patterson interview, April 7, 2010.

Courtroom 401 was a windowless jewel box: author observation, jury instructions video.

Patterson felt at home here: Patterson interview, April 7, 2010.

High-profile, time-consuming cases: Patterson interview, September 29, 2009.

sending Timothy Robinson and Michael Coleman: Florida Department of Corrections, www.dc.state.fl.us/activeinmates/details.

The key to success in the courtroom: Patterson interview, April 7, 2010.

Patterson felt confident: Patterson interview, April 7, 2010.

He always used three-by-five note cards: Patterson interview, April 7, 2010.

Dressed in a purple sweatshirt: Daniel Wells testimony, Bonifay trial, July 15, 1991, p. 213; Kelly Bland testimony, July 16, 1991, p. 2.

Patterson called sixteen witnesses: Bonifay trial, July 15, 1991.

Cliff avoided looking at Patrick: Barth letter, February 27, 2010.

Patterson asked him what happened: Clifford Barth testimony, trial transcript excerpts, July 16, 1991, p. 8.

asked Cliff if Patrick appeared to be stoned: Barth testimony, transcript excerpts, July 16, 1991, p. 16.

This dude is trying to get me killed: Patrick Bonifay letter, March 1, 2009.

Patrick felt no sense of betrayal: Bonifay letter, November 18, 2009.

But when Cliff testified that Patrick: Bonifay letter, March 1, 2010.

"Oh, don't worry about it," he said: Bonifay letter, November 20, 2009.

Patrick had lost all confidence in and respect for: Bonifay letter, November 20, 2009.

The trial of James Patrick Bonifay: Bonifay trial, July 16, 1991, p. 364.

Stokes knew that: Ted Stokes interview, April 8, 2010.

"At the onset let me remind you: Bonifay trial, July 16, 1991, pp. 371–72.

Patterson did play chess: Patterson interview, April 7, 2010.

"You should not convict the defendant at this stage*: Bonifay trial, July 16, 1991, pp. 378–79.

Archer, who, dressed in a blue shirt and white tie: Robin Archer trial excerpts, July 17, 1991, p. 29.

Stokes, who had advised Patrick not to take the stand: Patrick Bonifay interview, April 5, 2010.

But in his mind, this was his last, and only: Patrick Bonifay interview, April 5, 2010.

"I want you to murder somebody": Bonifay testimony, Robin Archer trial excerpt, July 17, 1991, p. 2.

"He came up to me and he was kind of giggling: Bonifay testimony, Archer trial excerpt, July 17, 1991, p. 7.

Patrick knew Lang had him in a lie: Patrick Bonifay interview, April 5, 2010.

"How much money was in that briefcase: Bonifay testimony, Archer trial excerpts, July 17, 1991, pp. 8–9.

Chapter 7. Life and Death

As she approached the witness stand: Crenshaw interview, April 8, 2010.

She felt revolted by how: Crenshaw interview, September 26, 2009.

Theresa was fifteen when she ran away: Crenshaw interview, September 26, 2009.

He seemed to emerge from her womb demanding things: Crenshaw interview, September 26, 2009.

Theresa, nervous and anxious: Crenshaw interview, April 8, 2010.

Her confusion over what to do: Patrick Bonifay school records, kindergarten to tenth grade.

To Theresa, this sounded like a teacher shirking: Crenshaw interview, September 29, 2009.

When another kid snatched a pencil: Crenshaw interview, September 29, 2009.

Theresa didn't know what to do: Crenshaw interview, September 29, 2009.

I didn't give birth to a monster: Crenshaw interview, September 29, 2009.

Theresa braced herself: Crenshaw interview, April 8, 2010.

I don't want to throw up: Crenshaw interview, April 8, 2010.

"Did you become aware of some: Crenshaw testimony, Bonifay trial, July 15, 1991, p. 451–52.

In a steady, forceful voice: Crenshaw interview, April 4, 2010.

the burglary of an auto-repair shop in Mississippi: Southhaven (Mississippi) Police Department incident report, May 5, 1990.

There was certainty, and defiance, in her voice: Crenshaw interview, April 4, 2010.

frustration began to replace the queasiness: Crenshaw interview, April 4, 2010.

Patterson had badgered her: Crenshaw interview, April 4, 2010.

Patrick listened to his mother's testimony: Patrick Bonifay letter, November 18, 2009.

Patrick hadn't expected his mother: Patrick Bonifay interview, November 14, 2008.

When it was his turn on the stand: Patrick Bonifay interview, April 5, 2010.

But on the stand, facing the jury: Patrick Bonifay interview, April 5, 2010.

The courage he had summoned to commit the murder: Patrick Bonifay interview, April 5, 2010.

"Did you want to kill the man?": Bonifay testimony, Bonifay trial, July 15, 1991, p. 467.

This public undressing of his childhood: Patrick Bonifay interview, April 5, 2010.

"I know that's a hard thing: Bonifay trial, July 15, 1991, pp. 470–71.

read the psychological evaluation: Lakeside Center files, 1979–91.

Nobody loves me: Patterson interview, September 29, 2009.

Patterson had doubts of whether the molestation: Patterson interview, April 7, 2010.

"You told your mother: Bonifay trial, July 15, 1991, p. 473–74.

"Who was the leader?": Bonifay trial, July 15, 1991, pp. 484–85.

Patterson saw no evidence of remorse: Patterson interview, April 7, 2010.

"Isn't it true the only thing you're sorry: Bonifay trial, July 15, 1991, pp. 486–87.

His answers confirmed in Patterson's mind: Patterson interview, April 7, 2010.

"And what did you do?: Bonifay trial, July 15, 1991, pp. 489–90.

The switch between sorrow and anger clicked: Patrick Bonifay interview, April 5, 2010.

"We have the defendant's mom: Bonifay trial, July 15, 1991, pp. 514–15.

In Florida, it takes a simple majority: American Bar Association, *The Florida Death Penalty Assessment Report*, September 2006, p. vi.

While the jury deliberated: Patrick Bonifay interview, April 5, 2010.

The prick: Patrick Bonifay interview, April 5, 2010.

Patrick exhaled, his head dropped: *Pensacola News Journal*, July 20, 1991.

Patrick's mother felt the sick: Crenshaw interview, April 8, 2010.

the whole thing looked staged: Killam interview, September 25, 2009.

Killam was threatened with contempt: Killam interview, September 25, 2009.

He believed the jury would find him innocent: Clifford Barth interview, October 2, 2009.

In early July, in a four-page letter: Michael G. Allen to Clifford Barth, letter, July 8, 1991.

He believed he had an agreement: Clifford Barth interview, October 2, 2009.

The night before his trial: Clifford Barth interview, October 2, 2009.

On the morning of August 27: Barth letter, April 26, 2009; Barth letter, February 27, 2010.

pleading with him to plea-bargain: Walter and Sheila Barth interview, May 7, 2009.

He didn't understand their fears: Barth letter, April 26, 2009.

"Your honor, I've discussed this matter: Barth hearing, August 29, 1991, pp 3–11.

Patterson wanted to wait: Killam interview, September 25, 2009.

Facing Eddie, who was seated at the defendant's table: Barth testimony, Fordham trial, August 27, 1991, p. 152; Tom O'Neal testimony, Fordham trial, August 27, 1991, p. 222.

"Who says crime doesn't pay?": Barth testimony, Fordham trial, August 27, 1991, p. 35.

to Eddie's thinking it was more damaging to Cliff: Eddie Fordham interview, January 29, 2010.

Eddie was eager: Eddie Fordham interview, January 29, 2010.

he was feeling nervous, anxious, and uncertain: Eddie Fordham interview, January 29, 2010.

They don't believe me: Eddie Fordham interview, January 29, 2010.

To Eddie, he looked like Superman: Eddie Fordham interview, January 29, 2010.

"I'm guilty of not thinking": Eddie Fordham testimony, Fordham trial, August 28, p. 112.

"He threatened you," Patterson said: Fordham trial, August 28, p. 97.

"And the reason you didn't testify: Fordham trial, August 28, 1991, p. 117.
"In their trials, why did I not want you to testify?": Fordham trial, August 28, 1991, p. 117.
In the give-and-take of the courtroom: Eddie Fordham interview, January 29, 2010.
"Yes, he did, but I'm sure: Fordham testimony, Fordham trial, August 28, 1991, p. 118–19.
"As a matter of fact," Patterson said: Fordham trial, August 28, 1991, p. 119.
He thought about all he had missed: Eddie Fordham interview, January 16, 2009.
He should get the death penalty: Eddie Fordham interview, August 29, 2009.
Alone in the room, he cried: Eddie Fordham interview, January 29, 2010.
He tried to read their faces: Eddie Fordham interview, January 29, 2010.
Diana Fordham cried out: Pensacola News Journal, September 19, 1991.
The next day, Patterson stood: Pensacola News Journal, August 30, 1991.
"He doesn't think he can convince the jury: Eddie Fordham letter, March 14, 2010.
Eddie Fordham stood before Judge Collier: Pensacola News Journal, September 19, 1991.
A tearful Eddie told the judge: Pensacola News Journal, September 19, 1991.
At his sentencing, Cliff stood stoically: Pensacola News Journal, September 19, 1991.
"Your honor, I would ask the court: Barth sentencing, September 18, 1991, p. 7.
"Well, I do want to state for the record: Barth sentencing, September 18, 1991, p. 8.
Collier sentenced Cliff: Barth sentencing, September 18, 1991, p. 9.
My life is over: Clifford Barth interview, October 2, 2009.
Pensacola News Journal published a letter: Pensacola News Journal, September 19, 1991.
"Nothing could be more heinous: Bonifay sentencing, September 20, 1991, pp. 7–8.
Archer stared straight at the judge: Pensacola News Journal, September 20, 1991.
All rode in silence: Eddie Fordham interview, February 27, 2009.
"Lake Butler Experience": Patrick Bonifay letter, March 16, 2009; Eddie Fordham interview, February 27, 2009.
Death row, what is that like?: Bonifay letter, March 16, 2009; Patrick Bonifay interview, September 25, 2009.

Chapter 8. Death Row

To Patrick, death row felt: Patrick Bonifay, letter, October 19, 2009.
A stainless-steel toilet: Florida Department of Corrections, www.dc.state.fl.us/oth/deathrow/index.
The cell was cold: Bonifay letter, October 19, 2009.
The cell's filth reminded him: Bonifay letter, November 20, 2009.
"How long before they kill us?": Patrick Bonifay interview, September 9, 2009; Bonifay letter, October 19, 2009.
The guards treated the death-row prisoners: Bonifay letter, October 19, 2009.
death-row prisoners feared for their sanity: Bonifay letter, November 20, 2009.
average death-row inmate in Florida: Florida Department of Corrections, www.dc.state.fl.us/oth/deathrow/index.
Patrick Bonifay noticed that some: Bonifay letter, November 20, 2009.
Patrick was a month into his death-row experience: Bonifay letter, October 19, 2009.
Jerome was fifteen when he and two other teenagers: Orlando Sentinel, July 17, 1991.
Florida hadn't executed anyone as young as Jerome: Orlando Sentinel, April 23, 1994.
At Jerome's sentencing: Orlando Sentinel, July 17, 1991.

On death row, Jerome didn't behave like an adult: Bonifay letter, October 19, 2009.

Chapter 9. State of Alarm

Gary Colley pulled the Chevrolet Cavalier: *Miami Herald*, September 14, 1995.
had lived together for seven years: *Ottawa Citizen*, March 14, 1999.
The couple was aware of attacks: *Ottawa Citizen*, March 14, 1999.
The I-10 rest stop, about thirty miles east: author observation.
For a moment she thought: *Ottawa Citizen*, March 14, 1999.
"Give it up! Give it up!": *Miami Herald*, November 16, 1994.
"I can't hear you," Jagger said: *The Independent* (London), November 16, 1994.
backing into a red Pontiac Bonneville: *Miami Herald*, January 24, 1995.
The .38-caliber bullet severed Colley's carotid artery: *Miami Herald*, November 16, 1994.
"Dip, man, dip!": *St. Petersburg Times*, November 17, 1994.
the headlines of British papers screaming: *St. Petersburg Times*, March 10, 1994.
it was Green: *Tampa Tribune*, February 19, 1995.
When legislators came back in February: *Miami Herald*, April 12, 2010.
Florida prosecutors charged seven thousand juveniles: "The Florida Experiment," 1.
unprecedented expansion of the prison system: *St. Petersburg Times*, October 10, 1994.
Florida was not alone: *New York Times*, May 10, 1994; *New York Times*, July 24, 1981.
the Florida Supreme Court ruled in Jerome Allen v. the State of Florida: Supreme Court of Florida, *Jerome Allen v. State of Florida*, March 24, 1994.
political scientist John J. Dilulio Jr.: John J. Dilulio, "The Coming of the Super-predators," *Weekly Standard*, November 27, 1995.
"On the horizon, therefore, are tens of thousands: Dilulio, "Coming of the Super-predators," 6.
Psychology professor Terrie E. Moffitt concluded: Elizabeth S. Scott and Laurence Steinberg, *Rethinking Juvenile Justice* (Cambridge: Harvard University Press, 2008), 16.
In the spring semester of 1995: Elizabeth Cauffman interview, July 12, 2010.
There was no consensus among the states: *Frontline*, "Juvenile Justice," www.pbs.org.
reminded some of Santa Claus: Cauffman interview, June 25, 2010.
Cauffman was a twenty-two-year-old graduate student: Cauffman interview, July 12, 2010.
Cauffman knew it wasn't a question about: Cauffman interview, July 12, 2010.
Cauffman argued for the older teenager: Cauffman interview, June 25, 2010.
What she found was some evidence: Laurence Steinberg and Elizabeth Cauffman, "Maturity of Judgment in Adolescence: Psychological Factors in Adolescent Decision Making," *Law and Human Behavior* 2 (1996): 267–69.
At first the data confounded her: Cauffman interview, June 25, 2010.
Cauffman and Steinberg published the findings of her dissertation: Cauffman interview, June 25, 2010.
they laid the foundation: Cauffman interview, June 25, 2010.
In 2001, Steinberg and Cauffman published their findings: Laurence Steinberg and Elizabeth Cauffman, "Adolescents as Adults in Court: A Developmental Perspective on the Transfer of Juveniles to Criminal Court," Social Policy Report, *Society for Research in Child Development* 15 (2001): 1–12.

released a study titled "Juveniles' Competence: Laurence Steinberg, Thomas Grisso, Jennifer Woolard, Elizabeth Cauffman, Elizabeth Scott, Sandra Graham, Fran Lexcen, N. Dickon Reppucci, and Robert Schwartz, "Juveniles' Competence to Stand Trial as Adults," Social Policy Report, *Society for Research in Child Development* 17 (2003): 1–14.

Steinberg and Scott published their rebuttal: Laurence Steinberg and Elizabeth Scott, "Less Guilty by Reason of Adolescence: Developmental Immaturity, Diminished Responsibility, and the Juvenile Death Penalty," *American Psychologist*, December 2003, 1013–17.

given the choice, adolescents were far more likely: "Less Guilty by Reason of Adolescence," Issue Brief 3, MacArthur Foundation Research Network on Adolescent Development and Juvenile Justice.

"The available evidence supports the conclusion: Steinberg and Scott, "Less Guilty by Reason of Adolescence," 1013–17.

"Dr. Cornell testified: Wal-Mart Stores Inc. Sandra Coker, Supreme Court of Florida brief of respondent, October 1997, pp. 9–10.

"Wal-Mart was the adult here": Text of the Argument, *Coker v. Wal-Mart Stores, Inc., Lawyer Weekly*, August 2, 2004, 19.

"Wal-Mart violated a federal law: Text of the Argument, *Lawyer Weekly*, 19.

"What did it take to kill Billy Wayne Coker?": Text of the Argument, *Lawyer Weekly*, 19.

In a decision that surprised Levin: Levin interview, March 4, 2011.

The law, the judges ruled, "was enacted to prevent: Wal-Mart Stores Inc. v. Sandra Coker, District Court of Appeal of Florida, First District, June 23, 1997, p. 2.

In 1997 the Florida Supreme Court upheld the ruling: Text of the Argument, *Lawyer Weekly*, 20.

Both teens believed that helping Sandra Coker: Levin interview, March 4, 2011.

Chapter 10. Transformation

Patrick declared that: Patrick Bonifay testimony, Huff hearing, February 26, 2001.

Patrick's own mother didn't believe him: Crenshaw interview, September 26, 2009.

Theresa believed the recanting: Crenshaw interview, September 26, 2009.

"This month, your honor: Bonifay testimony, Huff hearing, February 26, 2001, pp. 88–89.

it could be grounds for overturning: Attorney Greg Farrar interview, April 11, 2011.

Theresa had doubts about her son's conversion: Crenshaw interview, September 26, 2009.

Patrick felt, for the first time: Patrick Bonifay interview, November 14, 2008.

Patrick began to question himself: Patrick Bonifay interview, November 14, 2008.

Patrick felt he had found the rain to extinguish the rage: Patrick Bonifay interview, October 17, 2008.

How can I be at odds with a belief that takes a man: Patrick Bonifay interview, October 17, 2008.

Six years into his death sentence: Patrick Bonifay interview, November 14, 2008.

Nabiyl Taqqi Ya'quib Musaaleh: Bonifay letter, August 28, 2008.

Patrick Bonifay as Nabiyl Musaaleh believed himself: Patrick Bonifay interview, April 5, 2010.

shed the tears of his ignorance at the grave: *Dallas Morning News*, April 20, 1997.

"Based on the Court's experience: Circuit Judge Michael Jones, February 24, 2004, cited by Supreme Court of Florida, *Robin Lee Archer v. State of Florida*, October 12, 2006, p. 9.

The judges and lawyers believe what they want: Bonifay letter, March 1, 2010.

I did what I could, Patrick told himself: Bonifay letter, March 1, 2010.

Cleo Douglas LeCroy: *Fort Lauderdale Sun Sentinel*, March 1, 1986.

Nathaniel Ramirez: *St. Petersburg Times*, March 2, 2005.

Chapter 11. Hope

The worst room in the house: Christopher Simmons letter, November 16, 2010.

brief and stormy marriage: Christopher Simmons' Petition for a Commutation, or Reprieve of, a Sentence of Death, 2002, p. 5.

On the street where they lived: Simmons' Petition for a Commutation, pp. 6–7.

Hayes attacked his son's acne: Simmons letter, November 16, 2010.

Christopher seethed with hatred and fear: Simmons letter, November 16, 2010.

Banished to the basement: Simmons' Petition for a Commutation, p. 7.

It was a mouse-infested, dank, musty-smelling: Simmons letter, November 16, 2010.

They owned the house, but they had to mortgage it: Simmons letter, November 16, 2010.

Hayes took him fishing, got drunk: Simmons' Petition for a Commutation, p. 9.

Hayes used to bring him along: Simmons' Petition for a Commutation, p. 9.

The first time he ran away, in 1994: Simmons' Petition for a Commutation, p. 10.

his mother seldom went looking for him: Simmons' Petition for a Commutation, p. 10.

By the time he was seventeen: Simmons' Petition for a Commutation, p. 11.

encouraged teenagers to commit crimes for him: Simmons' Petition for a Commutation, p. 20.

provided the juveniles with a parent-free place: Simmons' Petition for a Commutation, 20–21.

Charlie and Christopher knew each other well: *St. Louis Post-Dispatch*, June 6, 2002.

left Moomey's trailer to burglarize a home: *Roper v. Simmons*, petitioner's brief, p. 3.

"Who's there?" she said: *Roper v. Simmons*, petitioner's brief, p. 4.

When Christopher walked into the bedroom: *Roper v. Simmons*, petitioner's brief, p. 4.

he killed some woman because the bitch saw his face: *Roper v. Simmons*, petitioner's brief, p. 5.

Christopher could see the police coming down the hall: Simmons interview, September 13, 2010.

Christopher was interrogated by police: American Bar Association, www.abanet.org/crimjust/juvjust/simmons.

the United States stood alone: *Roper v. Simmons* ruling, March 1, 2005, p. 14.

Former President Jimmy Carter: *Los Angeles Times*, July 20, 2004.

"The adolescent's mind works differently from ours: *Roper v. Simmons*, amicus brief of the American Medical Association, et al., July 23, 2009, p. 2.

Brain-imaging technology and performance tests: *Roper v. Simmons*, amicus brief of the American Psychological Association, July 19, 2009, pp. 9–10.

the adolescent limbic system is bristling with receptors: AMA amicus brief, July 23, 2009, p. 12–15.

Gilfoyle's aha moment: Nathalie Gilfoyle interview, July 2, 2010.

may be misdiagnosed: APA amicus brief, July 23, 2009, p. 3.

"Assessments of such severe antisocial behaviors: APA amicus brief, July 23, 2009, p. 3.

From his cell on death row: Patrick Bonifay interview, October 17, 2008.

thirty-one men and one woman were executed: Florida Department of Corrections, www.dc.state.fl.us/activeinmates/deathrowroster.

On Starke's death row: Florida Department of Corrections, www.dc.state.fl.us/activeinmates/deathrowroster.asp.

Patrick became convinced: Patrick Bonifay interview, October 17, 2008.

Kennedy cited three major differences: *Roper v. Simmons*, Supreme Court ruling, p. 15.

"The reality that juveniles still struggle: *Roper v. Simmons*, p. 16.

"Whether viewed as an attempt: *Roper v. Simmons*, p. 17.

"When a juvenile offender commits a heinous crime: *Roper v. Simmons*, p. 20.

"It is proper that we acknowledge: *Roper v. Simmons*, p. 24.

"I'm out of here.": Patrick Bonifay interview, October 17, 2008.

Am I in a dorm full of Crips?: Patrick Bonifay interview, October 17, 2008.

it's starting already: Bonifay letter, March 1, 2009.

Patrick felt like a man in shock: Patrick Bonifay interview, October 17, 2008.

But in the exercise yard: Patrick Bonifay interview, October 17, 2008.

I have to go from here to there: Patrick Bonifay interview, October 17, 2008.

In his first months at Jackson: Patrick Bonifay interview, October 17, 2008.

"Nabiyl! People are staring at you: Bonifay letter, March 1, 2009.

Patrick formed his own walls within the prison: Patrick Bonifay interview, October 17, 2008.

He had always thought of himself as an exceptional fighter: Patrick Bonifay interview, October 17, 2008.

When the thought surfaced, he buried it: Patrick Bonifay interview, January 30, 2009.

"Former Death Row Inmate Earns Silver Star: Patrick Bonifay interview, January 30, 2009.

A poor boy who once talked of a briefcase full of half a million dollars: Patrick Bonifay interview, January 30, 2009; Bonifay letters, February 19, 2009, December 20, 2008, January 12, 2009.

I'll die in prison: Patrick Bonifay interview, January 30, 2009.

In his darkest days: Patrick Bonifay interview, January 30, 2009; Bonifay letter, December 20, 2008.

Epilogue

Eddie Fordham stopped wearing a watch: Eddie Fordham interview, November 2, 2009.

"Hey, happy Father's Day": transcript of recorded phone call, June 21, 2009.

the Fordhams moved on: Larry Fordham Sr. interview, March 7, 2009.

On his chest are small scars: Eddie Fordham interview, November 2, 2009.

Sandra Faye Coker and Diana Fordham: Diana Fordham interview, March 7, 2009.

"It's just a short bridge.": Diana Fordham interview, March 7, 2009.

Sandra asked that Eddie be denied: Sandra Faye Coker interview, April 8, 2010.

His mother cried as they embraced: Eddie Fordham letter, April 9, 2009.

Brandy wore a silver necklace with a pendant: Eddie Fordham letter, April 9, 2009.

They didn't talk about it that day: Brandy Bartol interview, May 29, 2009.

couldn't help but imagine: Larry and Diana Fordham interview, March 7, 2009.

On the way back to his cell: Eddie Fordham letter, April 9, 2009.

On the first weekend in October: author observation.

what amounts to solitary confinement: Clifford Barth interview, March 9, 2009.

At Holmes he lifted weights: Barth letter, April 16, 2009.

In the dayroom, where the men crowded: Barth letter, June 16, 2009.

In tiny, neat, printed letters: Barth letter, April 5, 2009.

Cliff is a man without definite plans: Clifford Barth interview, March 9, 2009.

Since his imprisonment in 1991: Barth letter, April 22, 2011.

"My supervisor has denied your request: Inmate Request form, September 14, 1999.

Cliff requested, and was granted: Barth letter, April 22, 2011.

When he allows himself to imagine a future: Clifford Barth interview, March 3, 2009.

Walter Barth blamed his wife: Walt and Sheila Barth interview, May 7, 2009.

In the 1990s, while still on death row: Saffiya Musaaleh interview, July 24, 2009.

Saffiya felt she loved him: Saffiya interview, July 24, 2009.

What am I doing here?: Saffiya interview, July 24, 2009.

He's some fine-ass white boy: Saffiya interview, July 24, 2009.

Patrick and Saffiya symbolically became husband and wife: Saffiya interview, September 27, 2009.

asked Saffiya if she would adopt the son: Saffiya interview, July 24, 2009.

Saffiya had become disillusioned: Saffiya interview, September 27, 2009.

He admonished her: Saffiya interview, July 24, 2009.

She had helped him publish: Saffiya interview, July 24, 2009.

Patrick blamed Saffiya for rewriting the book: Patrick Bonifay letter, October 19, 2009.

After fifteen years with Patrick: Saffiya interview, September 27, 2009.

Patrick believed he belonged among them: Patrick Bonifay interview, September 25 2009.

"Sentencing an adolescent to life: Bryan Gowdy oral argument, November 9, 2009, p. 3.

They live in a small, blue frame house: author observation.

He calls them his poor man's patents: Patrick Bonifay interview, April 5, 2010.

"You're going to see this on the Outdoor Channel: Patrick Bonifay interview, April 5, 2010.

The plans for Country Boy Enterprises': Crenshaw interview, April 8, 2010.

Crain's Cemetery is a parched open graveyard: author's observation.

Coda

"Mrs. Coker, I have a theory: Eddie Fordham letter, July 4, 1991.

Bibliography

Anderson, Chris, and Sharon McGehee. *Bodies of Evidence: The True Story of Judias Buenoano Florida's Serial Murderess.* Secaucus, N.J.: Carol Publishing Group, 1991.

Bowden, Earle. "Lacey Collier: From Navy Skies to Federal Bench." *Pensacola Magazine*, March 1993, 12–13.

Butterfield, Fox. *All God's Children: The Bosket Family and the American Tradition of Violence.* New York: Vintage Books, a Division of Random House, 1995.

Dilulio, John J. "The Coming of the Super-predators." *Weekly Standard*, November 27, 1995.

Fordham, Larry E., Jr. "Fast Eddie and the Crossroads of Choice: A True Story for Teens." Copyright 1991–2007.

"Less Guilty by Reason of Adolescence." Issue Brief 3, MacArthur Foundation Research Network on Adolescent Development and Juvenile Justice.

Schiraldi, Vincent, and Jason Ziedenberg. "The Florida Experiment: Transferring Power from Judges to Prosecutors." *Criminal Justice Magazine* 15, no. 1 (2000), http://www.americanbar.org/publications/criminal_justice_magazine_home/crimjust_cjmagazine_15_1_schiraldi.html.

Scott, Elizabeth S., and Laurence Steinberg. *Rethinking Juvenile Justice.* Cambridge: Harvard University Press, 2008.

Steinberg, Laurence, and Elizabeth Cauffman. "Maturity of Judgment in Adolescence: Psychological Factors in Adolescent Decision Making." *Law and Human Behavior* 20 (1996): 249–69.

————. "Adolescents as Adults in Court: A Developmental Perspective on the Transfer of Juveniles to Criminal Court." Social Policy Report, *Society for Research in Child Development* 15 (2001): 1–12.

Steinberg, Laurence, Thomas Grisso, Jennifer Woolard, Elizabeth Cauffman, Elizabeth Scott, Sandra Graham, Sandra Lexcen, N. Dickson Reppucci, and Robert Schwartz. "Juveniles' Competence to Stand Trial as Adults." Social Policy Report, *Society for Research in Child Development* 17 (2003): 1013–17.

Steinberg, Laurence, and Elizabeth Scott. "Less Guilty by Reason of Adolescence: Developmental Immaturity, Diminished Responsibility, and the Juvenile Death Penalty." *American Psychologist*, December 2003, 1009–17.

Jeff Kunerth is an award-winning journalist with more than 35 years' experience as a reporter, writer, and teacher. He is the product of the Iowa State University journalism department and Goucher College's MFA program in creative nonfiction. He and his wife, Gretchen, live in Altamonte Springs, Florida, and they are the authors of *Florida's Paved Bike Trails*.